W9-ANU-289

R01374 72019

OTHER TITLES IN THE GREENHAVEN PRESS LITERARY COMPANION SERIES:

AMERICAN AUTHORS

Maya Angelou
Stephen Crane
Emily Dickinson
William Faulkner
F. Scott Fitzgerald
Robert Frost
Nathaniel Hawthorne
Ernest Hemingway
Arthur Miller
Eugene O'Neill
Edgar Allan Poe
John Steinbeck
Mark Twain
Walt Whitman
Thornton Wilder

AMERICAN LITERATURE

The Adventures of
   Huckleberry Finn
The Adventures of Tom
   Sawyer
Black Boy
The Call of the Wild
The Catcher in the Rye
The Crucible
Death of a Salesman
Ethan Frome
Fahrenheit 451
A Farewell to Arms
The Glass Menagerie
The Grapes of Wrath
The Great Gatsby
Of Mice and Men
The Old Man and the Sea
One Flew Over the Cuckoo's
   Nest
Our Town
The Pearl
The Scarlet Letter
A Separate Peace
To Kill a Mockingbird
Twelve Angry Men

THE GREENHAVEN PRESS
Literary Companion
TO AMERICAN LITERATURE

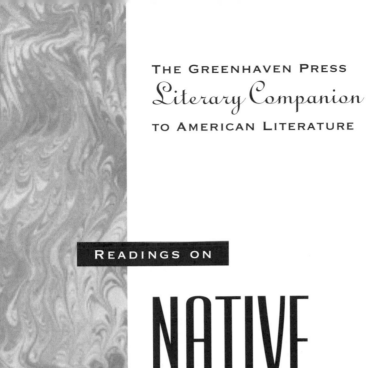

READINGS ON

NATIVE SON

Hayley R. Mitchell, *Book Editor*

David L. Bender, *Publisher*
Bruno Leone, *Executive Editor*
Bonnie Szumski, *Series Editor*

Greenhaven Press, Inc., San Diego, CA

Every effort has been made to trace the owners of copyrighted material. The articles in this volume may have been edited for content, length, and/or reading level. The titles have been changed to enhance the editorial purpose. Those interested in locating the original source will find the complete citation on the first page of each article.

Library of Congress Cataloging-in-Publication Data

Readings on Native Son / Hayley R. Mitchell, book editor.
        p.   cm. — (The Greenhaven Press literary
companion to American literature)
    Includes bibliographical references (p.   ) and index.
    ISBN 0-7377-0320-2 (alk. paper). —
ISBN 0-7377-0319-9 (pbk. : alk. paper)
    1. Wright, Richard, 1908–1960. Native son. 2. Afro-
Americans in literature. I. Mitchell, Hayley R., 1968–   .
II. Series.

PS3545.R815 N3435   2000
813'.52—dc21   99-053746
                                                         CIP

Cover photo: Archive Photos
Library of Congress, 32

Copyright ©2000 by Greenhaven Press, Inc.
PO Box 289009
San Diego, CA 92198-9009
Printed in the U.S.A.

"As I contemplated Bigger and what he meant, I said to myself: 'I must write this novel, not only for others to read, but to free myself of this sense of shame and fear.'"

—Richard Wright

CONTENTS

Chapter 1: The Art of *Native Son*

FOREWORD

The story's bare facts are simple: The captain, an old and scarred seafarer, walks with a peg leg made of whale ivory. He relentlessly drives his crew to hunt the world's oceans for the great white whale that crippled him. After a long search, the ship encounters the whale and a fierce battle ensues. Finally the captain drives his harpoon into the whale, but the harpoon line catches the captain about the neck and drags him to his death.

A simple story, a straightforward plot—yet, since the 1851 publication of Herman Melville's *Moby-Dick*, readers and critics have found many meanings in the struggle between Captain Ahab and the whale. To some, the novel is a cautionary tale that depicts how Ahab's obsession with revenge leads to his insanity and death. Others believe that the whale represents the unknowable secrets of the universe and that Ahab is a tragic hero who dares to challenge fate by attempting to discover this knowledge. Perhaps Melville intended Ahab as a criticism of Americans' tendency to become involved in well-intentioned but irrational causes. Or did Melville model Ahab after himself, letting his fictional character express his anger at what he perceived as a cruel and distant god?

Although literary critics disagree over the meaning of *Moby-Dick*, readers do not need to choose one particular interpretation in order to gain an understanding of Melville's novel. Instead, by examining various analyses, they can gain numerous insights into the issues that lie under the surface of the basic plot. Studying the writings of literary critics can also aid readers in making their own assessments of *Moby-Dick* and other literary works and in developing analytical thinking skills.

The Greenhaven Literary Companion Series was created with these goals in mind. Designed for young adults, this unique anthology series provides an engaging and comprehensive introduction to literary analysis and criticism. The essays included in the Literary Companion Series are chosen for their accessibility to a young adult audience and are expertly edited in consideration of both the reading and comprehension levels of this audience. In addition, each essay is introduced by a concise summation that presents the contributing writer's main themes and insights. Every anthology in the Literary Companion Series contains a varied selection of critical essays that cover a wide time span and express diverse views. Wherever possible, primary sources are represented through excerpts from authors' notebooks, letters, and journals and through contemporary criticism.

Each title in the Literary Companion Series pays careful consideration to the historical context of the particular author or literary work. In-depth biographies and detailed chronologies reveal important aspects of authors' lives and emphasize the historical events and social milieu that influenced their writings. To facilitate further research, every anthology includes primary and secondary source bibliographies of articles and/or books selected for their suitability for young adults. These engaging features make the Greenhaven Literary Companion Series ideal for introducing students to literary analysis in the classroom or as a library resource for young adults researching the world's great authors and literature.

Exceptional in its focus on young adults, the Greenhaven Literary Companion Series strives to present literary criticism in a compelling and accessible format. Every title in the series is intended to spark readers' interest in leading American and world authors, to help them broaden their understanding of literature, and to encourage them to formulate their own analyses of the literary works that they read. It is the editors' hope that young adult readers will find these anthologies to be true companions in their study of literature.

INTRODUCTION

On the day before the publication of *Native Son*, Richard Wright's editor, Edward Aswell, wrote to Wright to express his congratulations and to reiterate the confidence he felt in the book's guaranteed success. "It is my conviction," he said, "that its publication will be remembered in years to come as a monumental event."[1] Indeed, the novel has been considered as just such an event.

Native Son, published in March 1940, was the first novel by an African American to be selected for the Book-of-the-Month Club, and it was the first novel by a black writer to achieve best-seller status. Today, the book is taught in high school English classes and in a variety of college-level American literature and African American studies courses. *Native Son* earned Wright a permanent place in the canon of American literature, and the book has lost none of its original power in its ability to shock even contemporary readers into awareness of the social plight of black Americans.

In Wright's day, early reviews of the novel focused on this power: It is a "shock to our sensibilities," critics wrote; it "throbs from the opening line, with a wallop propelled to the end"; it "is a book which takes you by the ears and gives you a good shaking, whirls you on your toes and slaps you dizzy against the wall."[2] Critical acclaim in both the popular and academic press kept *Native Son* on the minds of the reading public. Ironically, library copies of the novel were in constant circulation, when a short fifteen years before, Wright, as a black man in the segregated South, was not allowed to check out library books for himself. Through his struggles, he had finally found success.

In addition to literary fame, biographer Keneth Kinnamon notes that another measure of Wright's success was that the book spurred sociological discussion of the lives of African Americans. Journalists referred to the novel in articles about poor housing conditions, and students held it up as a "revelation of social injustice and a demand for change."[3] In this light, Kinnamon says, "Wright made a cogent as well as a moving case against white racism"[4] which "altered the social as well as literary sensibilities of many of its readers."[5] The novel continues to do so today.

The essays in this volume explore the literary and social forces at work in *Native Son* by examining writing techniques, characters, the power of setting, and themes such as religion, racism, and violence. Some contemporary critics continue to explore Wright's craft from his use of grammatical structure to the imagery in his work. Other critics focus on issues such as the influence of mass culture in the novel, the archetypes of its characters, the effects of its gothic setting, or the function of violence in the book. Readers will find that these topics and many others in this collection offer a varied and exciting introduction to criticism on Richard Wright and *Native Son.*

NOTES

1. Quoted in Keneth Kinnamon, "How *Native Son* Was Born," in James Barbour, ed., *Writing the American Classics.* Chapel Hill: University of North Carolina Press, 1990, p. 228.

2. Quoted in Kinnamon, "How *Native Son* Was Born," p. 225.

3. Kinnamon, "How *Native Son* Was Born," p. 225.

4. Kinnamon, "How *Native Son* Was Born," p. 225.

5. Kinnamon, "How *Native Son* Was Born," p. 227.

Richard Wright: A Biography

Growing up in poverty in the racist South at the start of the twentieth century, Richard Wright was an unlikely candidate for literary fame. A onetime Communist and eventual expatriate, his life was one of both intense struggle and great professional acclaim. He became, against immense odds, America's first best-selling black author. Critically acclaimed for his writing, his work has influenced generations of African American writers and readers of all races.

Struggle at an Early Age

Richard Wright was born on September 4, 1908, in Roxie, Mississippi, to Nathan Wright, a sharecropper, and his wife Ella, a schoolteacher. Though humble, these beginnings might have afforded the young Richard a comfortable lifestyle and the same opportunities (though segregated) for education and advancement available to other black children of his day. However, abandoned by his father at an early age and shuttled between extended family members, the comforts of home and community did not materialize during Richard's early life. Rather, his early years were a constant struggle against poverty and the hunger that accompanies it, family disharmony, and the racism of the American South.

Although both his parents were employed, when Ella delivered her second child, Leon Alan, in September 1910, the Wrights found they could not afford to keep their farm running as well as take care of the boys. To lessen the financial burden, Richard's mother moved a year later with her sons to Natchez to live with her mother. Nathan, in the meantime, remained separated from the family, working odd jobs, until he secured a position with a sawmill. This move was the first of many during Richard's childhood.

In light of his history of struggle, it seems fitting that the first early memory of this period, recounted in Wright's autobiography, *Black Boy*, unhappily symbolizes much of his later strife. While living in his grandmother's house, Richard, who was nearly four years old at the time, set fire to her kitchen curtains, then hid underneath the house to avoid punishment. His convalescing grandmother needed to be evacuated, and his mother panicked when Richard could not be found. When he was discovered, she beat him severely.

Wright biographer Michel Fabre explains that this experience was the first of many in childhood that caused Richard great frustration, as he regarded his severe punishment as a form of betrayal. "It not only seriously inhibited his independent spirit," Fabre writes, "but also caused him to doubt his relationship to his mother. How could the source and object of all love turn into a fury, capable of punishing him so painfully and rejecting him so totally? This episode brutally shattered the emotional security he had derived from the exclusive affection of his mother."[1]

ABANDONED BY FATHER, LIVING IN SHAME

While Richard questioned his relationship with his mother, he also grew estranged from his father, who had been only a sporadic presence in his life up until now. When the family did regroup and moved to Memphis, Tennessee, in 1913, instead of becoming closer to his father, Richard resented him for working at night and sleeping during the day, an arrangement that forced Richard and his brother to remain quiet during daylight hours. Then, in 1914, when Richard was age six, Nathan sealed his son's negative opinion of him forever by abandoning his family for another woman.

Nathan's departure and his subsequent refusal to pay Richard's mother enough child support for them to live on was a source of shame for the family. Ella was shamed by being forced to take Nathan to court and also by asking her sons to beg him for money when the court's judgment was in Nathan's favor. Richard, in turn, was ashamed to have to face his father and his mistress, but he had enough pride at age six to refuse his father's money after he had begged for it. Richard and his brother also had a sense of being outsiders. They were different from other children, their mother said, because now they did not have a father.

Although Richard's mother worked as a cook for whites to support the family during this time, she was unable to make ends meet. The family suffered from hunger for the first time in their lives. Wright biographer Addison Gayle notes that this hunger exacted both a physical and mental toll on Richard:

> To young Richard Wright, hunger brought home the full im-
> pact and consequences of the absence of the father he had
> grown to hate. For the first time in his life, the pain of hunger
> became constant, overpowering. It was unexplainable, frus-
> trating, nerve-wracking. Whole days passed with scarcely
> more than bread and tea. The ability to play freely left him.
> He grew tense, nervous, morose.[2]

Richard spent much of his time wandering the streets,
thinking about food and his new responsibilities as the man
of the house. It was also during this period that Richard
learned to fight to stick up for himself on the streets of Memphis and when, as he notes in *Black Boy*, he became somewhat of a drunkard after acquiring a taste for alcohol served
to him for the amusement of patrons at local taverns.

A BRIEF OPPORTUNITY

Richard felt additional shame in his poverty when he attended school for the first time at age eight. He remained a
shy boy at Howe Institute, and he was fearful of speaking in
front of others. Despite feeling inferior to the other children,
Richard did gain a few friends, from whom he learned a
number of obscenities whose usage would later get him into
trouble at home as well as in the neighborhood. Just as he
was starting to settle into a normal pattern at school, however, another crisis hit home. As would be the case with all
his attempts at formal education, Richard's attendance at
Howe Institute was interrupted. On this occasion, the cause
was the sudden illness of his mother in 1916.

Richard dropped out of school to care for his sick mother,
unaware that this was the first of a number of illnesses that
would debilitate her for most of the rest of her life. Ella's illness crippled the already poverty-stricken family to the
point of destitution. She subsisted on charity for a short
while, but then was forced to put Richard and his brother in
a local orphanage for more than a month because she could
not care for them.

His brief stay at the orphanage served as another source
of frustration and fear for Richard. The other children were
bitter and vindictive, and he felt mistreated by the orphanage director, Miss Simon, after he refused to allow her to
adopt him. When he tried to run away, he was returned by a
white police officer and beaten by Simon. Wright was not to-

tally abandoned by his mother at this time. She did visit the boys frequently, beseeching them to have patience with her as she worked to improve her health and save enough money to allow them to leave Memphis.

Once Ella had saved enough money for the trip, she moved with the boys first to spend the summer with her parents, now living in Jackson, Mississippi, and then to Elaine, Arkansas, to live with Richard's Aunt Maggie and Uncle Silas Hoskins. Richard and his brother enjoyed the change of scenery during their summer in Jackson, but they lived under the rule of their devoutly religious grandmother, against whose strict authority Richard would soon rebel. When the family moved to Elaine, Richard felt more at home in his Aunt Maggie's house and enjoyed the attention of his Uncle Hoskins. This brief happy period was cut short by a racial killing that deeply affected Richard and changed the direction of his life yet again.

A LESSON IN RACISM FORCES ANOTHER MOVE

Silas Hoskins owned a saloon frequented by black sawmill workers in Elaine. In 1917, shortly after Richard moved in with his aunt and uncle, Silas was shot in his saloon after ignoring the threats of white men who wanted to take over his property. Upon hearing that threats had been made on the entire family, Maggie and Richard's family fled to West Helena immediately. Before this incident, Richard was wary of whites; on the streets he had heard rumors of black men being beaten or killed by whites, but this was the first time he was aware of racism's direct effects. The result was a new fear and hatred of whites: "This was as close as white terror had ever come to me and my mind reeled," Wright writes in his autobiography. "Why had we not fought back, I asked my mother, and the fear that was in her made her slap me into silence."[3]

Moving frequently after the death of Silas Hoskins, between 1917 and 1919 the Wrights first settled again with Ella's mother in Jackson, but then set off on their own to West Helena, where Ella suffered a stroke. Now paralyzed and unable to care for her sons, Ella accompanied her mother back to Jackson, Leon joined Aunt Maggie in Michigan, and Richard moved in with his Uncle Clark and Aunt Jody in Greenwood, Mississippi, near Jackson.

Although Richard was well provided for in Greenwood,

he felt ill at ease in his uncle's home. He became overly sensitive to criticism directed at improving him, and he suffered feelings of guilt over his mother's suffering. Richard began to sleepwalk and seemed on the verge of a nervous breakdown after learning that a young boy had died in the room he was now occupying. Afraid of being in the house and becoming more and more difficult for his aunt and uncle to handle, the overwrought Richard was sent again to live with his mother and grandmother in Jackson, where he would spend the remainder of his adolescence.

ADOLESCENCE IN JACKSON

Between 1920 and 1923, Richard attended three schools, worked a variety of odd jobs, and further developed an interest in reading that had been piqued previously by magazine adventure stories. Richard attended the first of the three schools in 1920, a Seventh-Day Adventist school in Huntsville, Mississippi. Although his grandmother believed the Adventist school would supplement the religious instruction he received at home, he clashed violently with his Aunt Addie, the devoutly religious teacher of his class.

Richard felt that the other children in Addie's class were dull and that the work was not challenging enough. Addie, on the other hand, felt threatened by Richard's boredom in class. She beat him in front of the other children to make an example of him, but Richard knew that the beating was without just cause. Later, when Addie tried to beat him at home, he defended himself with a knife, learning, Michel Fabre writes, "to overcome the authority of the family, discovering that violence would also earn him respect in the adult world."[4]

Rather than return to the Adventist church for the subsequent school year, Richard was allowed to attend Jim Hill School, a public school in Jackson. He entered the school as a fifth grader but was soon advanced to sixth grade despite his relative lack of previous schooling compared with other children. Richard took joy in his success at the school and made friends among his classmates. In addition to these social successes, however, during his years at Jim Hill, Richard's poverty was apparent to everyone. His entire family was now living in poverty after having spent the last of their savings on medical specialists for Ella, who showed no signs of recovering from her paralysis. Richard's clothes were in tatters, he could not immediately afford books and other school supplies, and he often went hungry.

To earn a little money for food and necessities, Richard delivered newspapers and worked with a traveling insurance salesman, two jobs he recalls with some shame in his autobiography. Richard enjoyed selling the newspapers for the magazine stories that they included. He would sneak these works into his grandmother's house, where he had been forbidden to read anything other than religious material. He soon quit his newspaper route in shame, however, upon learning from the father of one of his friends that the paper was run by supporters of the Ku Klux Klan.

Richard's job as an insurance salesman assistant likewise filled him with shame when he discovered the exploitation of Negro families he was obliged to make sales calls to in the Delta. In the Delta the plantation system flourished. The illiterate blacks there worked in the cotton fields and were forbidden education. Richard was depressed by the squalor of entire families living in one-room shacks. Addison Gayle notes that it was here that Richard "found unmistakable evidence of the human spirit crushed, of the desire for freedom not dormant but non-existent—and he hated it," referring to the people there as a "bare bleak pool of black life."[5]

After his summer of work, Richard returned to school in 1922, entering seventh grade at the Smith-Robertson Public School. He continued to earn money for books, food, and clothes by doing odd jobs such as running errands for whites. Over the year his interest in pulp fiction and magazine stories deepened, and he read every story that he could get his hands on. Among Richard's favorites were detective stories in *Flynn's Detective Weekly*, Agatha Christie stories, Zane Grey's *Riders of the Purple Sage*, Jack London's adventure stories, and Edgar Allan Poe's detective works. These and other tales, still forbidden in his household, planted the seeds for Richard's first creative efforts, which would soon be made public.

BITTERSWEET SUCCESS

During his eighth-grade year, when Richard was fifteen, he wrote his first short story, "The Voodoo of Hell's Half-Acre," which was serialized in three installments in the black newspaper *Jackson Southern Register* in 1924. As Wright describes it in *Black Boy*, the purely atmospheric story concerns a villain who is after an elderly widow's home. The character of the villain is based on a neighborhood bully, James Biggy Thomas. It was a small first accomplishment, but one that Richard was proud of just the same, and something he erroneously thought might earn him respect among his family and peers.

Although Malcolm Rogers, the editor of the newspaper, was impressed by Richard's writing and urged him to submit more work, neither Richard's family nor his community encouraged his literary pursuits. Grandmother Wilson riled against Richard's use of "hell" in his title and believed that his soul was stricken for writing lies; as Wright notes in his autobiography, her opinion of all fiction was that it was the devil's work.

Richard's mother likewise condemned his work, worrying aloud whether the story might prevent him from acquiring a good job in the neighborhood. In addition, Richard's friends did not understand why he would want to write in the first place; his work clearly had no value to those around him. Despite the lack of encouragement he received from others and his disappointment over not being paid for his work, Kinnamon writes that Wright was pleased to see his work in print. "The pleasures of authorship as well as the delights of reading," he says, "had become for Wright a tactic for survival."[6]

Besides his brief literary accomplishment, Richard continued to do well in his studies and in 1925 he graduated valedictorian of his ninth-grade class at Smith-Robinson School. A minor disagreement occurred at the time between Richard and the assistant principal, W.H. Lanier, who had prepared a speech for him that would be sure not to offend important white school officials in attendance at the graduation. Richard refused to read the prepared speech, however, and gave one of his own. He graduated, Kinnamon says, "tense, defiant, estranged from his black world and fearful of the white world he was about to encounter, but taking a grim satisfaction in his own integrity."[7]

After graduating with his ninth-grade class at age sixteen, Richard resolved to forgo further public education and to leave the Deep South for Memphis, Tennessee. Instinctively, he seemed to know that life in Jackson could offer him little more than he already had. "A black boy was boxed in by four alternatives in the deep South," biographer Margaret Walker writes:

If he was not in school and had no job, he had to be either in
the army or in jail. These were his options. Vagrancy or the
semblance of what is put on the face of it was not tolerated in
a black male. No standing on the corner, day or night was allowed, and black youths congregating in gangs on street corners were in open defiance of the law whether they knew this
or not.[8]

With one hundred dollars in his pocket—most of which he
had acquired through dishonest dealings at a local movie
house—and a single suitcase in hand, Richard said good-bye
to his mother, assuring her that he was leaving on his own ac-
cord, not because he was in some kind of trouble with Jackson whites. It was a proud moment for him, and although he
was heading into unknown territory, he felt a new sense of
freedom as he left his adolescence and Jackson behind.

WORKING IN THE WHITE WORLD

Soon after arriving in Memphis, Richard was able to draw
from previous experience working in an optical shop to get a
job at the Merry Optical Company as an assistant and deliv-
ery boy. He lived frugally during this time, eating poorly to
save enough to send money home for his mother and brother
to join him. In addition to his struggle to get by on his meager wage, Richard found that moving to the North had not al-
leviated his inner turmoil about whites. While whites in the
North were not violent toward blacks, racial tensions in his
workplace were palpable. "Race hatred permeated the atmosphere," Gayle writes, "but it was buried under preten-
sions of urban smugness, covert, rendered more often
through symbolic actions rather than overt ones."[9]

In the community, segregation was less obvious than under
the strict Jim Crow laws of the Deep South, but Richard's freedom was still limited. His local library, for example, was
closed to blacks. To indulge his passion for reading, Richard
was forced to borrow books from whites until a white
coworker lent him the use of his library card. Even then,
Richard was forced to forge a note to the librarian, requesting
that he be allowed to deliver the books to his employer.

In this episode, much recounted in Wright biographies,
and also explained in some detail in *Black Boy*, Richard is
known to have written, "Dear Madam: Will you please let
this nigger boy have some books by H.L. Mencken."[10] The
derogatory language that Richard chose for this note proves
that he was deeply aware of the racist attitude of whites in

Memphis, and that his position as a "nigger boy" was broadly accepted in the community at large.

DESIRING AND ACCOMPLISHING GREATER THINGS

The more widely Richard read in Memphis, the greater his desire to achieve literary success of his own. In addition to Mencken, writers such as Sinclair Lewis, Mark Twain, Joseph Conrad, Theodore Dreiser, and others inspired him to work toward leaving the South completely and moving somewhere that afforded him more opportunity. His chance came between 1927 and 1928, when after saving enough money for his mother and brother to join him in Memphis, he set out for Chicago with his Aunt Maggie, to again find work and save to bring his family farther north.

In Chicago, Richard worked at a number of odd jobs before landing a part-time position with the postal service. After years of poor nutrition, however, he could not pass the physical exam (at age twenty, he weighed less than the required 125 pounds) to work there full-time. Regardless of this fact, he was making more money than he ever had in the past and was able to both save and eat regularly, and he soon had enough money for his mother and brother to move up from Memphis.

By the spring of 1929, Richard had gained enough weight to pass the postal health exam, and he began to work as a substitute clerk and mail sorter. His financial security was short-lived due to the impending stock market crash and the subsequent depression, which would put him out of work again in less than a year, but this period was an important one for Richard.

His family was secure in a larger apartment, and he was free to read and write more regularly. Richard also sought out the company of those who would better appreciate his literary yearnings than his family and immediate community by briefly attending meetings of black literary groups. He did not feel as though he fit in well with these groups, however, as he sensed their desire to achieve success as writers was less than his own. He accomplished more in writing in solitude at home.

In addition to a number of short stories at the time, he also began working on his first novel, called *Cesspool*, which ultimately would become *Lawd Today*, his last novel, published posthumously. Of his work at this time Wright says,

"My writing was more an attempt at understanding than self-expression. A need that I did not comprehend made me use words to create religious types, criminal types, the warped, the lost, the baffled; my pages were full of tension, frantic poverty, and death."[11]

THE DEPRESSION AND COMMUNISM

In the spring of 1930, Richard lost his postal job in the aftermath of the stock market crash. He worked for a short time selling burial insurance to blacks, but, dismayed by the dishonesty of the profession, he quit to take whatever odd jobs he could find. Eventually ending up on state relief, Richard later worked as a porter for the Michael Reese Hospital, mopping floors and cleaning the cages of experimental animals, and then for the South Side Boy's Club and Federal Negro Theatre.

Although his work life was unfulfilling and his family could now ill afford their large apartment, Richard did gain another small success in his literary life. His second publication, the short story "Superstition," appeared in *Abbott's Monthly Magazine*, a black journal. Richard wrote the story specifically for the magazine's audience, and he was later ashamed that it contained no worthy social or political commentary. What distressed him more at the time, however, was that, due to the depression, he did not receive the thirty dollars promised him for the story.

During the depression years, many of Richard's writer friends developed an interest in Communist literary groups and encouraged him to join. He remained skeptical at first, however, having seen the activities of the League of Struggle for Negro Rights, a radical Communist group in the African American community. Of this group Wright commented in *American Hunger*, part two of his autobiography:

> I liked their courage, but I doubted their wisdom. The speakers claimed that Negroes were angry, that they were about to rise and join their white fellow workers to make a revolution. I was in and out of many Negro homes each day and I knew that the Negroes were lost, ignorant, sick in mind and body. I saw that a vast distance separated the agitators from the masses, a distance so vast that the agitators did not know how to appeal to the people they sought to lead.[12]

Despite these feelings, Richard did eventually join his friends in attending another Communist group, the John Reed Club, in 1932.

In 1932 Richard was working as an insurance salesman and a streetcleaner. He was forced to move his family into a dirty tenement. Depressed by these conditions, his affiliation with the literary John Reed Club in 1933 allowed him to escape the atmosphere of work and home. Here, he felt a sense of community that he had rarely felt elsewhere in his life.

THE JOHN REED CLUB INFLUENCE

Controlled by the Communist Party, the John Reed Club solicited black members during the depression, and its members welcomed Richard courteously and treated both him and his writing with respect. He was not required to join the Party to attend club meetings, but the preamble of the club insisted, Kinnamon notes, that "the interests of all writers and artists should be identified with the interests of the working class."[13]

In addition to the companionship Richard gained through his club attendance, he also found a new outlet for his writings. The group was affiliated with the Communist Party magazine *New Masses* as well as *Left Front,* a journal devoted to writers in the early stages of their career. Richard was soon regularly publishing his poems and short stories in these and other leftist journals.

As Richard's publication credits in these journals grew between 1933 and 1934, he also became more involved in communism. Fabre explains that although Richard "was somewhat torn between his new sympathies and his mother's religious beliefs, he came to see in Marxism an organized search for truth about the life of oppressed peoples, and this convinced him that the Communists were sincere."[14] Thus, Richard joined the Communist Party after he was elected executive secretary of the Chicago John Reed Club in 1934; he also served as a member of the literary board of *Left Front.*

Much to his disappointment, Wright's involvement with the John Reed Club was cut short by the Party's decision to disband the clubs in the summer of 1934 in an effort to focus on political pursuits. Wright remained active in these other more political arenas. In addition, he was one of sixty-four writers who founded the American Writers' Congress in 1935. The first conference of the congress took place in New York in the spring of 1935; though the event was run by the Communist Party, non-Communist writers were in attendance as well. Wright attended and gave a speech on "The Isolation of the Negro Writer," in which he stated:

> Some of the more obvious results [of isolation] are lack of contact with other writers, a lack of personal culture, a tendency toward escape mechanisms of ingenious, insidious kinds. Other results of his isolation are the monotony of subject matter and becoming the victim of a sort of traditional Negro character.[15]

Although Wright was becoming more well known for his writing, he still faced racism daily. Even while attending the conference, he was refused a room in a "whites only" hotel in Harlem. Despite this racial setback at the conference, his activity there led to new work, as he was soon hired by the Federal Writers' Project to research the history of Illinois and of the Negro in Chicago.

MAKING A NAME FOR HIMSELF

In addition to working for the Federal Writers' Project, Wright organized the Communist Party–sponsored National Negro Congress, held in Chicago in February 1936. He was specially selected by the Party to preside over sessions on black history and culture. These literary activities gave Wright a chance to meet other prominent African American writers of the day, such as Langston Hughes, and encouraged him to continue to write extensively.

In November, his own writing efforts paid off when his short story "Big Boy Leaves Home" appeared in the anthology *New Caravan*, where it attracted critical attention. For the first time his serious efforts at fiction were noticed outside the Communist Party by the white press. Although the story did receive praise in Socialist papers such as the *Daily Worker* and *New Masses*, it was also lauded in the *New York Times* and the *Saturday Review of Literature.*

With the success of "Big Boy Leaves Home," Richard began to turn away from his poetry, which had appeared regularly in numerous journals, to focus on short-story writing. And while much of the fiction he sent out for publication still came back rejected, in 1937 Richard decided to turn down a permanent position with the postal service to move to New York City to pursue his writing career.

In Chicago, Richard had begun to feel stifled by the Communist Party. He even withdrew his national Party membership at one point, while remaining connected to his local chapter. Now in New York, however, he found the Party to be more liberal and intelligent, so he reinstated his Party membership.

Soon after reestablishing his Party ties, Richard became the Harlem Bureau editor of the Party newspaper, the *Daily Worker*. Additionally, he helped launch the magazine *New Challenge,* which was in fact the continuation of a previously established journal titled *Challenge*. Richard also lent his writing talents to *New Masses* and the New York City Writers' Project, and he worked on what was soon to become his first published book of stories.

That book was *Uncle Tom's Children: Four Novellas.* The theme of each of the novellas was racial conflict and violence, a theme that Richard would continue to explore in later works. When the book was published in 1938, it received some harsh criticism, but mostly wide acclaim. The work received favorable reviews in both the scholarly and popular press and was praised by both black and white critics alike. Richard's story "Big Boy Leaves Home," which was a part of the collection, also won a five-hundred-dollar first prize from the prestigious *Story* magazine. Other stories in the collection won individual awards as well, and within a year, Richard was awarded a Guggenheim fellowship, which gave him financial stability and allowed him the necessary time to complete his first published novel, *Native Son.*

A BRIEF MARRIAGE

As the publication of *Uncle Tom's Children* and various awards marked his emergence into literary celebrity, Wright was moving toward marriage. He just needed to decide which of two women he was going to marry: Dhimah Rose Meadman, a white classical dancer and divorcée with a two-year-old son, or Ellen Poplar, a white member of the Communist Party. He chose Dhimah, marrying her in August 1939, with African American writer Ralph Ellison serving as best man.

The couple soon moved to Mexico with Dhimah's mother and son. Life in Mexico was said to be cheaper than in New York, and the new family hoped to escape the tensions of the early months of World War II (America had not yet joined the war). The arrangement seemed ideal for Wright, who could write and live cheaply. What Richard found in Mexico, however, was that he was quickly swept up into an active social life, entertaining American visitors in his ten-room villa.

Marriage to Dhimah did not meet Richard's expectations, as Fabre explains:

> He had hoped to have more time with his wife, only to find that she reveled in this worldly and artistic circle of which she was the center. He suddenly discovered that Dhimah was preoccupied with herself, whereas he would have liked her to be more completely devoted to him. He now saw her as just as indolent and insensitive to him as she was to their servants and the natives.[16]

Thus, unsuited to Dhimah's material lifestyle, Richard returned to the States alone in the summer of 1940 after just three months in Mexico. The pair divorced before the end of the year.

NATIVE SON

If *Uncle Tom's Children* stirred up good press for Wright, *Native Son*, a novel of social protest, created a tidal wave of acclaim. When the book was published in March 1940, it became the first featured selection of the Book-of-the-Month Club by an African American writer. The national attention the novel received as a result boosted sales to over a quarter million copies in three weeks, making Wright the first bestselling black author in America. He soon found himself the subject of radio and magazine interviews as well, and he was sought after for lectures nationwide.

Clearly, Wright's social criticism through the vehicle of his violent main character, Bigger Thomas, struck a chord with American readers, especially African Americans. Black poet James Baldwin claimed, for example, "No American Negro exists who does not have his private Bigger Thomas living in his skull."[17] While there are numerous similarities between Richard and Bigger, however, the fictional character is not based entirely on himself. In his essay "How Bigger Was Born," Wright explains that the character was a conscious composite of five southern black men he had known throughout the years. "All of them were rebellious defilers of the Jim Crow order, and all of them suffered for their insurgency,"[18] Kinnamon says. In Wright's words, "they were shot, hanged, maimed, lynched, and generally hounded, until they were either dead or their spirits were broken."[19]

In short, Bigger Thomas was real to Richard's readers because he was drawn from the harsh realities of Negro life, albeit realities that some Americans in the 1940s were possibly unaware of and many were unwilling to face. Reactions to the book were bound to be controversial, and Wright was especially concerned about its reception in the black press. Black readers, Fabre notes, were often torn between their pride over Wright's literary rise to fame and their disgust over the dislikable Bigger Thomas:

> The choice of such an antisocial black protagonist, so near the bottom of the social ladder, was bound to confirm the racists' prejudice that the black man was a beast lusting after white women. The more enlightened understood, however, that the novel might bring at least the liberal whites to realize the gravity of the problem.[20]

Richard's fears of negative black community reaction, despite some dissenting critics, were assuaged when James Ivy, speaking for the National Association for the Advancement of Colored People (NAACP), found nothing to criticize in his work.

Just as Bigger Thomas was a composite of real people and real problems, the landscape of *Native Son* also grew out of Richard's memories of living or working in slum conditions in the South. In this book, and, in fact, in much of Wright's work, autobiography simmers just below the fictional veneer. Kinnamon writes, "The details of the Chicago environment in the novel have a verisimilitude that is almost photographic."[21] Ernie's Kitchen Shack of the novel, for example, is a slightly disguised restaurant called the Chicken Shack, once owned by one Ernie Henderson.

Also true to life, Richard's Communist politics are manifest throughout the novel. As Kinnamon explains, the courtroom arguments of the novel are leftist, equating prejudice with economic exploitation. "Communist ideology provided [Wright] with an intellectual instrument with which to render meaningful the personal and social material of the novel," Kinnamon writes:

> The nice balance of subjective and objective elements prevents *Native Son* from being either a purely personal scream of pain, on the one hand, or a mere ideological tract on the other. It is a work of art as well as an expression of protest, and an examination of the way in which Wright organized his narrative, presented his characters, and employed symbols to enrich his meaning reveal a high degree of artistic seriousness.[22]

Although some Communist reviewers claimed *Native Son* gave readers misleading impressions about the Party and was not sufficiently propagandist, which they felt Wright was duty-bound to be in all his writings, he was clearly rewarded elsewhere for his sense of artistry. In addition to finding its way into the esteemed Book-of-the-Month Club, the novel received critical praise from both the literary and popular press. Indeed, one reviewer likened Wright to John Steinbeck and Theodore Dreiser, writers he had admired during the early stages of his self-directed literary education. Another reviewer was so impressed with the work he found it "difficult to write temperately of a book which abounds in such excitement, in so much that is harrowing and in so profound an understanding of human frailty."[23]

Not all of the critical reaction to *Native Son* was positive, however. Reviewer David L. Cohen's reaction, for example, was one of the angriest: "Justice or no justice, the whites of America simply will not grant to Negroes at this time those things that Mr. Wright demands. The Negro problem in America is actually insoluble. . . . Hatred, and the preaching of hatred and incitement to violence can only make a tolerable relationship intolerable."[24]

While *Native Son* had its critics in Cohen and others, the favorable press outweighed the negative. Had he not gone on to write future novels, with *Native Son* Richard Wright had made his indelible mark in the history of American and Afro-American literature.

More Literary Success, Wedding Bells, and Breaking Party Ties

The year 1941 was a busy one for Wright. Amid the monetary and critical success of *Native Son* the previous year, Orson Welles had purchased the rights to turn the novel into a Broadway production, with Wright and writer Paul Green as scriptwriters. In addition to working like mad to make last-minute revisions to the play at the beginning of the year, Richard also completed, with coauthor Edwin Rosskam, *Twelve Million Black Voices: A Folk History of the Negro in the United States*, which was published the same year.

Native Son, the play, opened on Broadway in March and ran through June for 115 performances in all. While the play and its actors received mostly good reviews in the press, it did not earn a profit and audiences were limited. Despite the fact that the play lost money, the good press continued to enhance Richard's literary reputation. "The important papers praised the play on artistic grounds," Fabre writes, "the Left hailed it on ideological grounds and because it represented an innovation for Broadway, and even the Communist press was mostly favorable."[25] Even Hollywood got in on the act when Metro-Goldwyn-Mayer Studios offered to buy the movie rights. Wright rejected the offer, however, as the studio hoped to produce the film with white actors in the leading roles.

In addition to his continuing literary success, Richard's personal life improved in 1941 as well when he was reunited with Communist Party member Ellen Poplar. The two married in March and moved into an apartment in New York. In April of the next year, their first daughter, Julia, was born.

Over the next three years, Richard continued to write for a variety of publications, and sections of his autobiography were accepted for publication by magazines such as the *Atlantic Monthly*. In these years he also gradually became less active in Communist activities, and in 1944 he broke from the Communist Party completely and published a two-part article about his experiences in the Party in the *Atlantic Monthly* titled, "I Tried to Be a Communist."

In the article, Richard condemned individual Party members for the ill treatment he felt he had received from them in his later years with the group. "The article questioned the sincerity of the Communists," Fabre writes, "and revealed the 'terrorist' methods used at the very heart of the Party toward the somewhat undisciplined members, emphasizing the total scorn for individual liberty which such disciplinary action betrayed."[26] Richard's article drew immediate criticism from Party members. Some members who had once been his friends now rejected him outright; others chose not to denounce him, but they would not defend him either.

BLACK BOY

As it turned out, Richard needed little defending, as the publication of his autobiography, *Black Boy*, guaranteed public favor. Regarding *Black Boy*, Wright says, "I wanted to give, lend my tongue to the voiceless Negro boys."[27] Published in 1945, *Black Boy: A Record of Childhood and Youth* was assured of success by becoming Richard's second book accepted for the Book-of-the-Month Club.

As Fabre writes, *Black Boy* forced the American reader to consider the South from the black man's point of view for the first time. Wright's book, however, not only criticized the racist whites of the South, it also condemned blacks over-eager to bend under the weight of the Jim Crow laws, and all those who strove to make "good Negroes," obedient, unquestioning black men, out of them.

Despite some criticism, *Black Boy* topped the best-seller list on April 29, 1945, just one month after its publication, and it remained there for a week. By the end of the year, it ranked fourth among all nonfiction sales; sales in translation were also strong, including in the Scandinavian countries, Brazil, and Palestine, among others. As an enduring testament to the book's success, *Black Boy* is included in high school and college curricula today.

A New Life in Paris

In 1946, amid the great success of *Black Boy*, Wright and his family were invited by the French government to take a month-long, all-expenses-paid trip to Paris. Wright, who had been wanting to make the trip for some time to visit expatriate friend and writer Gertrude Stein, accepted ecstatically. On arriving in France, Wright found that he was treated more as a celebrity and intellectual than he had been treated in the States.

Walker writes, "He was now an international figure welcomed on another continent and treated not merely as a worthy human being, but somebody special, illustrious, and held in reverence with no thought of condensation because of race, color, or creed."[28] It was the kind of reception that one can imagine Wright had dreamed about when he wrote his first story in eighth grade, and in Europe he felt a freedom he had never experienced in America. In sum, he felt Europeans were more cultured and, most importantly, more accepting of interracial couples. Richard had finally found a place where he truly felt at home. It is not surprising, therefore, that he and Ellen decided to move their family to Paris permanently in the summer of 1947.

Wright continued to expand both his career and his family while in Paris. His second daughter, Rachel, was born in January 1949, and he also finished the screenplay of *Native Son* in the same year. As he was unable to interest Hollywood in the script without agreeing to changes he found unacceptable, Wright and his partners sold the screenplay to European producers. Deciding to play the lead character, Bigger Thomas, himself, Wright remained closely connected with the production of the project, which filmed in both Chicago and Argentina.

Filming of *Native Son* wrapped up in June 1950 after a number of financial difficulties and other delays. The film finally opened in Buenos Aires in 1951, where it was met with triumphant reviews. Reaction was similar throughout Europe. In America, however, it was a different story. American critics were unenthusiastic about both the acting and editing. Wright nonetheless defended the film, blaming its failure in America on censors who demanded thirty minutes of the film be cut before its June 16 premiere. Some theaters even refused to show the film at all.

THE LITERATURE OF WRIGHT'S LATER YEARS

Between 1953 and 1960, Richard continued to live and write in Paris. The first of his books published during this time was *The Outsider*, appearing in 1953. Though it was sold as fiction, the book, like most of his work, was autobiographical in nature. In America, Richard's new book was widely reviewed, as the press there were anxious to view the effects of expatriation on his writing. The reviews were mixed.

Richard Wright

Always at work on another project, Wright did not let negative reviews of *The Outsider* affect his work. In the year of its release, he obtained a special visa to visit the Gold Coast of Ghana to gather material on Africans for his book *Black Power: A Record of Reactions in a Land of Pathos*, which was published in 1954. Another of Richard's novels, *Savage Holiday*, his only novel with all white characters, was published the same year. This novel was considered pulp fiction, published as a paperback, and did not receive serious attention from the academic or literary press. Richard's regular publishers rejected the book, and he worried that they would not accept any new work from him that did not explore issues of race.

As in the previous year, Richard did not let his literary success, or lack thereof, prevent him from moving forward with other plans. As before, he traveled, but this time to Spain with interest in another writing project. In 1955, the following year, Richard's travels took him to Indonesia, where he attended the Bandung Conference with numerous world leaders of Asia and Africa. The conference attendees discussed Third World problems and issues of racism and colonialism.

In 1956, Richard published his account of the conference, *The Color Curtain: A Report on the Bandung Conference.* His new book, *Pagan Spain,* based on his travels in Spain, also appeared in 1956 as he began a lecture tour of several European countries. Neither work sold well, however, and both soon went out of print until the 1970s, when Wright's work was repopularized among American college students.

Wright published more work in 1957 with *White Man, Listen!* a collection of lectures warning against continuing racism in America. The black press immediately praised the work, but the popular press criticized the work severely, calling him moralist and ungrateful for his previous success in America. Whatever the critical response, Walker writes that the publication of this book represented the end of a cycle in Wright's life. "It represents his ten years of lecturing and traveling over Europe, Africa, and Asia," she says. "It also ends the ten years in Paris that have been overflowing with productivity. In ten years he had written nine books, traveled thousands of miles, and given dozens of lectures."[29]

THE FINAL YEARS

Although Wright wrote and published until his unexpected death, his last three years in Paris were not especially happy ones. Though they did not divorce, Wright and Ellen had been estranged since the filming of *Native Son,* and he felt their marriage was essentially over, as Ellen had taken the girls to live in England to continue her career as a literary agent. Additionally, Wright felt harassed by the American government about his former Communist associations, and in January 1959 his mother died in Mississippi. Wright himself suffered a bout of amoebic dysentery at the time.

Wright seemed to be suffering both financially and professionally. Since his later works did not sell well and his earlier, successful books were now out of print, his royalties dwindled. He was forced to take on small writing projects, such as writing reviews for jazz albums. Things did not improve. Wright's feelings of rejection and discouragement multiplied, in fact, when he was unable to sell his novel *Island of Hallucinations,* which remains unpublished today.

Wright's last novel published in his lifetime represented his continued move away from European issues and focus on American life. This book, *The Long Dream,* was published in 1958. It was the first in a projected trilogy about Mississippi that he hoped would rekindle critical interest in his work, but like much of his later work, the book received poor reviews and did not sell well. Likewise, a 1960 stage adaptation of *The Long Dream* opened on Broadway but closed in a week after poor reviews.

Wright's last literary activity was in 1960, when he prepared more than eight hundred of his haiku for publication and began work on a new novel. *Eight Men,* a collection of short stories, was also ready for publication. It was published posthumously in 1961.

On November 28, 1960, Richard Wright died of a heart attack at age fifty-two. He was cremated with a copy of *Black Boy* on December 3 in Paris. The American press, though critical of his later work, mourned his untimely death and referred to him as a great American writer. Today, as readers discover Wright's novels, biographer Michel Fabre suggests that

> we must not forget that Richard Wright was attempting more than entertainment or even political enlightenment. Uncertainly at times, but more often quite consciously, he was grappling with a definition of man. Although his solitary quest ended prematurely and did not allow him to find one, his achievement as a writer and a humanist makes him, in the Emersonian sense, a truly "representative man" of our time.[30]

NOTES

1. Michel Fabre, *The Unfinished Quest of Richard Wright,* trans. Isabel Barzun. New York: William Morrow, 1973, p. 10.

2. Addison Gayle, *Richard Wright: Ordeal of a Native Son.* New York: Anchor Press, 1980, pp. 9–10.

3. Quoted in Keneth Kinnamon, *The Emergence of Richard Wright.* Urbana: University of Illinois Press, 1972, p. 10.

4. Fabre, *The Unfinished Quest of Richard Wright,* p. 38.

5. Gayle, *Richard Wright,* p. 27.

6. Kinnamon, *The Emergence of Richard Wright,* p. 37.

7. Kinnamon, *The Emergence of Richard Wright*, p. 35.
8. Margaret Walker, *Richard Wright: Demonic Genius*. New York: Warner, 1988, p. 38.
9. Gayle, *Richard Wright*, p. 43.
10. Quoted in Fabre, *The Unfinished Quest of Richard Wright*, p. 65.
11. Quoted in Gayle, *Richard Wright*, p. 55.
12. Quoted in Gayle, *Richard Wright*, p. 89.
13. Quoted in Kinnamon, *The Emergence of Richard Wright*, p. 51.
14. Fabre, *The Unfinished Quest of Richard Wright*, p. 97.
15. Quoted in Kinnamon, *The Emergence of Richard Wright*, p. 64.
16. Fabre, *The Unfinished Quest of Richard Wright*, p. 204.
17. Quoted in Kinnamon, *The Emergence of Richard Wright*, p. 119.
18. Kinnamon, *The Emergence of Richard Wright*, p. 120.
19. Quoted in Kinnamon, *The Emergence of Richard Wright*, p. 120.
20. Fabre, *The Unfinished Quest of Richard Wright*, p. 179.
21. Kinnamon, *The Emergence of Richard Wright*, p. 121.
22. Kinnamon, *The Emergence of Richard Wright*, p. 126.
23. Quoted in Kinnamon, *The Emergence of Richard Wright*, p. 144.
24. Quoted in Gayle, *Richard Wright*, p. 120.
25. Fabre, *The Unfinished Quest of Richard Wright*, p. 216.
26. Fabre, *The Unfinished Quest of Richard Wright*, p. 255.
27. Quoted in Fabre, *The Unfinished Quest of Richard Wright*, p. 252.
28. Walker, *Richard Wright*, pp. 198–99.
29. Walker, *Richard Wright*, p. 290.
30. Fabre, *The Unfinished Quest of Richard Wright*, p. 531.

CHARACTERS AND PLOT

THE CHARACTERS

Bigger Thomas is the central character of *Native Son*. He is twenty years old, stifled and disgusted by the Chicago tenement where he lives with his family. Bigger is frustrated by segregation and full of hatred for whites who have the material possessions and opportunities not afforded him in the ghetto. He uses violence to exercise power within his own community and to revolt against the privileged white society.

Mrs. Thomas, Bigger's mother, does not cater to Bigger's frustrations. She wants him to get a job and stay out of trouble, and she has little faith that blacks will rise above segregation. She turns to religion as a means of escape from poverty and the horror of Bigger's crimes.

Vera Thomas, Bigger's younger sister, appears infrequently in the novel. Constantly afraid of her surroundings, even in her own home, she symbolizes fear and victimization in the novel.

Buddy Thomas is Bigger's younger brother; like Vera, he has only a very minor role in the novel. Although frustrated and ashamed of his living conditions, unlike Bigger he accepts life under Jim Crow laws and is unwilling to step out of place.

Bessie Mears is Bigger's girlfriend, but readers do not get a sense of a true romantic relationship between the two. She is a lower-class girl struggling to survive by working long hours cooking for a white household. She turns to Bigger for escape from her dull life and bleak future through alcohol and sex.

G.H., *Gus*, and *Jack* are Bigger's friends. They appear only briefly in the novel and are peripheral to the plot. Bigger's feelings about white oppression are highlighted in his conversations with the boys, however, and his propensity for violence is shown when he beats Gus.

Mr. Dalton is the rich white man who serves as Bigger's benefactor by offering him a job in his home. He symbolizes the hypocrisy of white power. While he donates large sums of money to Negro charities, he is also secretly the slum landlord of the very tenement that Bigger despises.

Mrs. Dalton is another character who symbolizes the white establishment. While she thinks she is a philanthropist for the black community, her physical blindness suggests that she is quite ignorant of the plight of blacks.

Mary Dalton is the sole heiress to the Dalton fortune. She represents the ultimate white taboo, the kind of woman Bigger could be hanged for being involved with, whether he rapes her or not. Although she is friendly toward Bigger, he senses she is insincere and shallow. Like her parents, she has no true sense of what it means to be a black man in segregated Chicago. Bigger kills her when he fears his safety is threatened and he is about to be caught alone with her in her room.

Peggy is the Daltons' white housekeeper. She gives Bigger duties around the house and tells him about the Daltons' history of helping black people.

Jan Erlone is Mary Dalton's Communist boyfriend. He also attempts to befriend Bigger, but Bigger does not trust him, seeing him only as another force of white oppression. Bigger tries to blame Jan for Mary's murder, and after Bigger is caught, Jan works to understand Bigger's motives for killing. At the end of the novel Bigger asks his attorney to "tell Jan hello." Calling Jan by his first name is symbolic of Bigger accepting Jan's friendship.

Britten is a private detective hired by Dalton to solve Mary's disappearance. He does not realize that Bigger is the murderer, but the questions he asks him foreshadow Bigger's later interrogation after his capture.

Buckley is the state attorney prosecuting Bigger's case. His passion to convict Bigger is driven more by political motives than by the facts of the case, and he is clearly prejudiced against all blacks. He sees Bigger as a beast, a symbol of all of society's wrongs.

Boris A. Max is Bigger's defense attorney. He is a Marxist Communist and a friend of Jan's. He argues that Bigger is a mistreated victim of his racist environment. While he makes a passionate plea for Bigger's case, Wright suggests that Max, too, is blind to what Bigger has become. He recoils from Bigger's acceptance of himself as a murderer at the end of the novel.

PLOT SUMMARY

Book I: Fear

The first section of *Native Son*, titled "Fear," begins with Bigger Thomas waking to the violent ringing of an alarm clock and his mother's screams for him to get out of bed. Before he and his family even have a chance to dress, he is forced to kill a rat that has ventured out from the wall. It is a bleak scene of poverty and darkness, symbolizing the quality of Bigger's life. As the scene continues, Mrs. Thomas pressures Bigger to accept a job he has been offered by the Dalton family. Bigger is clearly of two minds about accepting the work, but knows he has few other choices.

Bigger leaves the apartment to meet his friends, who lament their lack of opportunities under white oppression. They make plans to rob a local white man's store, but they do not follow through. Bigger is agitated by the knowledge that he could never get away with robbing Blum, the white man. Even in crime there are ultimate taboos for blacks; robbing a white man is one, and raping a white woman is another, a crime punishable by death. Bigger resents the injustice of being able to rob his own people because the white police do not care enough to follow up on those crimes. In addition to resentment and hatred, it is important to understand that what Bigger feels most toward the white world is fear.

It is fear that causes Bigger to take his knife and his gun with him to the Daltons' on his first day as a chauffeur. The plush atmosphere of the Daltons' home further alienates him, reminding him of the material things blacks cannot acquire and the places they are not allowed to go. When Bigger is introduced to the Daltons' daughter, Mary, soon after entering the house, his past social conditioning in viewing the white woman as taboo causes him to hate her immediately. Mary, on the other hand, is oblivious to the social codes that instill so much fear in Bigger, who is suspicious of her friendly behavior.

Bigger's first task as a chauffeur is to drive Mary to a lecture in the evening. He is surprised when she directs him to pick up her Communist boyfriend, Jan, instead. Jan, like Mary, offers Bigger his friendship, but Bigger cannot see either of them as more than proponents of white oppression. Mary and Jan want to eat with Bigger in a black restaurant, and later they share alcohol with him while he drives them around the park.

Bigger drops Jan off at his car and returns to the Daltons' with Mary, who is too drunk to walk to her room on her own. He is forced to half-carry her to her bed. Once in her bedroom, Bigger is trapped by the appearance of the blind Mrs. Dalton, who comes in to check on Mary. Knowing full well the legal implications of being found in a drunken white woman's bedroom, Bigger panics and covers Mary's face with a pillow so that she will not speak up and give away his presence. Out of fear for his own safety, he accidentally smothers her.

In a panic, Bigger must now dispose of Mary's body. He carries her to the furnace in the basement and prepares to burn her. The horror intensifies as he must first decapitate her so that the body will fit into the furnace. After accomplishing the deed, he slips home and falls quickly asleep in his bed, a sense of relief and power surging through him.

Book II: Flight

The focus of Book II is the solution of Mary's murder and the apprehension of Bigger. Bigger awakes the morning after the murder to the stunning realization that he has killed a white woman. He wonders how this act has outwardly changed him. Though he is worried that his family will learn of his deed, he considers himself a real man in the aftermath of the murder. His self-esteem is bolstered by the knowledge that his friends would consider him a hero if only he could brag about his deed.

Bigger returns to the Dalton house to maintain a normal appearance. He remains cool when the family discovers Mary's disappearance and questions him about the events of the evening. Later, he leaves the Dalton home to visit his girlfriend, Bessie. Bessie is quick to discern that all is not right with Bigger. She figures out that he has harmed Mary, and Bigger hatches a plan for a ransom note, claiming that Mary has been kidnapped.

Bigger returns to the Daltons' after visiting Bessie and is questioned further about Mary's disappearance by the Daltons and their private investigator, Mr. Britten. Bigger tries to implicate Jan in the evening's events, but when Jan is called to the house, he denies having seen Mary after their ride in the park. In this scene Bigger benefits from Mr. Dalton's hatred for Communists, as Dalton does not accept Jan's story, thinking Jan knows more than he lets on. Bigger later pulls a gun on Jan in the street when Jan approaches him to talk about Britten's harassment.

Back at Bessie's, Bigger writes the ransom note. Bessie is frightened and says she will not go through with Bigger's plans as she slowly realizes that Bigger has actually killed Mary. He threatens her and forces her to ride on the street-car with him to show her the proposed drop-off point for the Dalton ransom money. He then sends Bessie home and continues to the Daltons', slipping the ransom note under the door before retiring to his quarters inside.

In the morning, the Daltons discover the ransom note and decide to issue a statement to newspaper reporters, who have already gathered in the basement to learn more about Mary's disappearance. Suddenly, while one of the reporters is helping remove ashes from the furnace to heat the cold basement, he discovers Mary's bones. Bigger sneaks out of the house during the commotion, returns to Bessie, and forces her out into the streets with him on the run. They enter an abandoned building and hide in a filthy third-floor room. As they prepare to sleep on the bed linens they have brought from home, Bessie attempts to ward off Bigger's sexual advances. He rapes her when she protests. Bigger then decides that Bessie is too much of a liability and kills her by bashing her head with a brick and throwing her into an airshaft, where she eventually freezes to death.

The remainder of Book II revolves around Bigger's flight from police in the Black Belt of Chicago's South Side. He is pursued by more than five thousand police officers. They search over a thousand homes while news reports of the killing convict Bigger of the murder before his capture. As he is pursued, his feelings of power from killing Mary and Bessie subside and the old fear of being a black man living under white oppression reemerges. Finally, he is dragged from his hiding place atop a water tower and taken to prison.

Book III: Fate

In Book III of *Native Son*, the essential action of the novel is complete. The final section focuses on Bigger's inner state and whether he will be able to draw some meaning out of his ordeal. Here, Bigger meets Boris Max, a Communist attorney and his public defender.

Max's plea to the court in Bigger's defense is really a civil rights speech for justice within the black and other minority communities. He argues that white oppression produced the violence of Bigger Thomas. Under the system of oppression, Max claims, Bigger is forced to rebel, and driven to murder. White society, argues Max, must acknowledge its role in Bigger's violent acts. Max suggests that to kill Bigger and to continue to oppress others will only create more rebellion.

Bigger falls into a kind of stupor for three days in his jail cell. He is not hopeful that Max will win his case for him, as he knows his fate has already been decided by his being born a black man in a racist, segregated society. When he awakens to full consciousness, he feels alone, unable to extract comfort from the friends and family who visit his cell, nor religious faith from the black reverend who encourages him to repent and find peace in God.

Later, he shocks Max with his admission that killing Mary was a positive thing because it forced him to get in touch with the fear and hatred inside himself. Max is unable to comprehend Bigger's growth as an individual in this light. Jan, however, is enlightened by Bigger's plight. He no longer sees him as a sociological project for his Communist politics, but as a human being affected by the white oppression for which Jan must now share some of the blame. The novel closes with Bigger's acceptance of himself as a murderer and the death sentence that will follow.

The Art of *Native Son*

Wright's Craft Is as Important as Content in *Native Son*

Joyce Ann Joyce

Joyce Ann Joyce, assistant professor of English at the University of Maryland, College Park, disproves earlier critics' claims that Wright pays more attention to the content or plot of *Native Son* than to the artistry of writing. She examines the role of alliteration, rhythm, sentence structure, and symbolism to show how Wright uses his craft to affect readers' emotions, reflect the thoughts and actions of his characters, and emphasize the tensions of a society split by racism in *Native Son*.

Because literary critics focus their interests on the social and political aspects of Richard Wright's works, they have seriously overlooked much of the ingenuity of Wright's craftsmanship. Published at the beginning of his serious career, *Native Son* remains the work that brought Wright his greatest success. Primarily a self-educated and self-trained artist, Wright, in his early works like *Native Son,* depends heavily upon the grammatical aspects of the craft of fiction—emphasis through repetition and traditional sentence structure. With a style that merges the creative processes of the novelist and the essayist, Wright successfully demands the attention of his readers and manipulates their sympathies through devices such as the alliterative sibilants that pervade the rat scene, the repetitive use of periodic and balanced sentence constructions, and the ubiquitous appearance of the words *black* and *white*. A concise examination of these aspects of Wright's artistry pales the supposition that Wright gives more attention to content than form by illuminating the intensity achieved through the interrelationship between Wright's subject matter and his expression of it.

Excerpted from "Style and Meaning in Richard Wright's *Native Son,*" by Joyce Ann Joyce, *Black American Literature Forum*, vol. 16, no. 3, 1982. Reprinted with permission from the African American Review.

ALLITERATION AFFECTS READERS' EMOTIONS

Two of *Native Son's* most distinguishing qualities are its emotive uses of alliteration and rhythm. The rat scene that begins the novel is impressive not only because a huge black rat attacks Bigger, but also because Wright uses language to manipulate the reader's emotions by making the scene move quickly through a series of alliterative action verbs that give the scene a hysterical quality. In this scene, which covers approximately three pages, Wright employs twenty different verbs of action beginning with the consonant *s.* The effect of these alliterative words is best exemplified by the passage that contains five forceful action verbs which capture the movement of the scene:

> "Goddamn!" Bigger whispered fiercely, whirling and kicking out his leg with all the strength of his body. The force of his movement *shook* the rat loose and it *sailed* through the air and *struck* a wall. Instantly, it rolled over and leaped again. Bigger dodged and the rat landed against a table leg. With clenched teeth, Bigger held the skillet; he was afraid to hurl it, fearing that he might miss. The rat *squeaked* and turned and ran in a narrow circle, looking for a place to hide; it leaped again past Bigger and *scurried* on dry rasping feet to one side of the box and then to the other, searching for the hole.

All intensifying the scene's ricocheting and tumultuous effect, the other verbs include *scrambled, stood, swept, sobbed, shoved, squealed, snagged, shouted, screamed, swung, skidded, sprang, stopped, scuttled,* and *searched.* No other section of the novel is more alliterative than this rat scene, in which these verbs are accompanied by the nouns *stove, sons, skillet, side, screak, step, song;* the participles *stocking, shaking, splintered,* and *searching;* the gerund *shattering;* and the adverb *slowly.* Through the function of alliteration in this scene, sound becomes an inextricable part of narrative action, subtly communicating the sensations of anxiety and fear.

Probably the most peculiar aspect of alliteration in *Native Son* is the ubiquitous presence of the sibilant *s.* Nonetheless, the reader will find occasional premeditated uses of other alliterative consonants such as those Bessie uses when she refers to herself as a "blind dumb black drunk fool." Here Wright has the alliterative stops *b* and *d* intensify character delineation. The function of all the other alliterative sibilants contrasts sharply with those of the rat scene. Whereas the alliterative verbs in the rat scene create a harsh, forceful effect that enhances the scene's rapid movement, the repetition of the sibilants in other passages has a soothing, calming effect. Such an effect serves as an emotional anodyne in a work with subject matter that offends the reader's sensibilities. An excellent example of the soft *s* sound to appease the reader's frustration appears in the extremely moving scene in which Max coerces Bigger to explain the reasons that he killed Mary Dalton. His extreme fear of whites coupled with his total inexperience at questioning his actions unleashes in Bigger an anxiety from which he seeks relief in a cigarette. In an alliterative line describing Bigger's actions while smoking, Wright's language assuages the reader's distress, incited by identification with Bigger's uneasiness. We are told that "Bigger sighed, shrugged his shoulders and sucked his lungs full of smoke." Numerous brief alliterative phrases such as "shooting star streaking across a black sky" and "down the slope, stopping still at his feet" achieve a similar effect throughout the novel.

Rhythm Reflects Bigger's Thoughts and Actions

Just as pervasive as the alliteration in *Native Son* is Wright's use of rhythm to enhance the work's emotional impact. Varying its sentence patterns significantly between periodic, balanced, and compound constructions, the novel achieves a lyrical ebb and flow that reflects the activity of Bigger's thoughts and actions. Integral parts of the novel's structure, descriptive participial phrases summarize past events, introduce Bigger's state of mind at given intervals, and, more importantly, justify Bigger's thoughts and actions for the reader. For instance, at the beginning of Book III, Wright uses a periodic sentence composed of a series of participial phrases to explain Bigger's "deep physiological resolution not to react to anything" during the initial stages of his confinement:

> Having been thrown by an accidental murder into a position where he had sensed a possible order and meaning in his relations with the people about him; having accepted the moral guilt and responsibility for that murder because it made him feel free for the first time in his life; having felt in his heart some obscure need to be at home with people and having demanded ransom money to enable him to do it—having done all this and failed, he chose not to struggle any more.

This long series of verbal phrases serves as a sharp contrast to the brief independent clause which offers the reader a sigh of relief, not only because it is brief, but also because it soothes the anxiety created by the phrases that introduce it.

Manipulative tools of the third-person-limited narrator, the novel's periodic sentences assure the reader's identification with the sudden nuances in Bigger's response to those around him. Intensifying the effect Wright achieves with the participial phrases, the novelist employs, in the jail scene in which all the figures who have influenced Bigger's life surround him, a series of elliptical clauses that build to a sensational crescendo and end with an emphatic independent clause. The rhythm in this section accomplishes an element of surprise. Traditionally, the phrases or dependent clauses of a periodic sentence progress through a rising rhythm, and the independent clause that follows maintains a falling movement. Wright sometimes varies this pattern. Instead of ending his jail-scene sentence with one independent clause, he ends it with two—the first momentarily abates tension while the second abruptly startles the reader. Construing Bigger's shame and frustration at being surrounded by his family, the Daltons, his friends, the district attorney, Jan, and Max, the narrator explains:

> While looking at his brother and sister and feeling his mother's arms about him; while knowing that Jack and G.H. and Gus were standing awkwardly in the doorway staring at him in curious disbelief—while being conscious of all this, Bigger felt a wild and outlandish conviction surge in him: *They ought to be glad!*

As he does here, Wright often italicizes those words he intends his readers to emphasize. By providing a precise and trenchant description of Bigger's instinctive awareness of the humiliation expressed on the faces of his family and friends, the elliptical clauses illuminate the contrast between Bigger's rebellious perception of life and the docility of his family and peers. Although the elliptical clauses emphasize the idea of the independent clause, they also depend on this clause to complete their meaning. Accomplishing an impressive balance between form and meaning, Wright in this scene has Bigger begin to perceive the interrelationship between his life and his family's.

Through their juxtaposition of contrasting or similar ideas in grammatically equal structure, the balanced and compound sentences also prove to be excellent embodiments of the interrelationship between form and meaning. After the scene in which Buckley cruelly tricks Bigger into signing a confession, Wright emphasizes Bigger's physical impotence as well as his eruptive emotions by using a series of balanced sentences that consistently juxtapose Bigger's physical helplessness with his strengthening of his emotional weapons. The narrator describes the agony Bigger experiences after having naively trusted Buckley:

> He lay on the cold floor sobbing; but really he was standing up strongly with contrite heart, holding his life in his hands, staring at it with a wondering question. He lay on the cold floor sobbing; but really he was pushing forward with his puny strength against a world too big and too strong for him. He lay on the cold floor sobbing; but really he was groping forward with fierce zeal into a welter of circumstances which he felt contained a water of mercy for the thirst of his heart and brain.

Heightening the reader's emotional response, Wright in this passage intertwines both rhythm and repetition. The repetitive independent clause that concretely describes Bigger's forced physical resignation serves as preface to the clauses that explain the abstract, overpowering sensations that paradoxically instigate and contrast with Bigger's weeping. The use of the balanced sentence in this section highlights Wright's premeditated stylistic techniques, for his balanced sentence—true to definition—places contrasting ideas inside similar grammatical structures, subtly controlling the reader's response.

COMPOUND SENTENCES ADD TO MEANING

As deliberate as the balanced sentences, the compound sentences that typify *Native Son* also become integral parts of the novel's content. Unlike the vacillating functions of the periodic and balanced sentences, there is a singleness of purpose to Wright's compound sentences: They punctuate the chasm between the novel's black and white worlds. In the "murder scene" immediately after Mrs. Dalton leaves the room and Bigger discovers that Mary is dead, the language describing Bigger's thoughts is a series of compound sentences stripped of most modifiers, suggesting the abrupt, matter-of-fact, mechanical treatment Bigger expects from the white world when it learns of Mary's death:

> He stood with her body in his arms in the silent room and cold facts battered him like waves sweeping in from the sea; she was dead; she was white; she was a woman; he had killed her; he was black; he might be caught; he did not want to be caught; if he were they would kill him.

The movement of Bigger's thoughts reflects the startling simplicity of the moral and physical codes that govern the interaction between the black and white worlds.

Further illuminating the mutual relationship between form and meaning, Wright uses a series of stark compound sentences not only to punctuate the aberrations of a caste system based on race, but also to explain the universal abstractions separating all individuals. Because the Daltons embody preconceived, stereotypical notions that characterize a racial society, they are unable to identify with Bigger's agony, spurred, as it is, by his shame at his black skin, and in turn they are also incapable of detecting his pretenses at ignorance and humility. After craftily answering Mrs. Dalton's questions about Mary's actions, Bigger feels very confident, realizing that her physical blindness merely reflects her lack of perception in relating to him. Punctuating not only the racial barrier that separates Bigger and Mrs. Dalton, but also the caste system that hampers their communication, the narrator describes Bigger's response to Mrs. Dalton:

> She must know this house like a book, he thought. He trembled with excitement. She was white and he was black; she was rich and he was poor; she was old and he was young; she was the boss and he was the worker. He was safe; yes.

As evidenced by the previous two passages, Wright reserves the use of the compound sentence and polysyndeton [the use of a number of conjunctions in close succession] to illumine his ideology. By stripping these compound sentences of all extraneous modifiers and by using excessive conjunctions, he accentuates the harsh realities of racially segregated communities.

THE SYMBOLISM OF *BLACK* AND *WHITE*

Strengthening this depiction of the emotional and physical dichotomy between the black and white worlds the novel describes, Wright gives the words *black* and *white* symbolic dimensions. Ubiquitous in the novel, *black* presages fear and humiliation while *white* warns of danger and insensitivity. The majority of the denotative uses of *black* and *white* unerringly and glaringly precede the appearance of every character while the more descriptive uses of these words escape the reader's critical eye, but subtly lure the reader into the novel's emotional world. These more elusive, connotative references to *black* and *white* limit themselves to descriptions of parts of the body and inanimate objects.

Two scenes readily demonstrate the metaphorical use of *black* to describe parts of the body. In the scene in which Bigger suffers intense humiliation when Jan asks him not to call him *sir,* the narrator manipulatively insists that the reader identify with Bigger's shame at his blackness: "Bigger paused, swallowed, and looked down at his black hands." And again when Bigger is angry with Bessie for her reluctance to agree to pick up the ransom money, the narrator construes Bigger's response: "His black open palm swept upward in a swift narrow arc and smacked solidly against her face." An interpretative guide, the narrator emphasizes not only the fear and humiliation Bigger experiences in the face of Jan's naive offering of friendship, but also his feelings of entrapment enhanced by Bessie's cowering.

Serving much the same function as the "black open palm" or "black hands" alluded to in the preceding paragraph, references to inanimate objects reflect Bigger's shame when in the presence of whites. When Buckley questions Bigger, attempting to persuade him to sign a confession, Bigger is extremely uneasy and is, some of the time, unable to meet Buckley's eyes: "He [Bigger] felt a hand touch his shoulder; he did not turn round; his eyes looked downward and saw the man's gleaming black shoes." The use of *black* here, intermingled with Bigger's looking down, underscores Wright's depiction of the emotional limitations of Bigger's degradation. Wright has Reverend Hammond—the epitome of a religious system that encourages feelings of shame and guilt—wear a black suit when he visits Bigger at the jail: "He stared at the man's jet-black suit and remembered who he was: Reverend Hammond, the pastor of his mother's church. And at once he was on guard against the man. He shut his heart and tried to stifle all feeling in him. He feared that the preacher would make him feel *remorseful"* (emphasis added). The preacher and his jet-black suit help Bigger to remember who he is.

Whereas *black* most frequently limits itself to those scenes in which Bigger is caught in the throes of fear and entrapment, *white,* embodied by the snow, indicates the blindness and insensitivity of the white world. When Bigger attempts to explain the image of himself that he sees in the white man's eyes, his words illustrate Wright's seemingly inadvertent use of *white:* "I knew that some time or other they

was going to get me for something. I'm black. I don't have to
do nothing for 'em to get me. The first white finger they
point at me, I'm a goner, see?" More than simply intensifying Bigger's fear, "white finger" functions as a reminder, jus-
tifying Bigger's helplessness. Having much the same effect
as in this scene, the language that describes the approach of
the two medical attendants who wheel Bessie's body into the
inquest appears superficially to lack a specific purpose: "He
[Bigger] looked and saw two white-coated attendants push-
ing an oblong, sheet-covered table through the crowd and
down the aisle." In the first passage Bigger indicates that the
white world is not concerned with his innocence and that
very mechanical laws govern the interactions between
blacks and whites. Similarly, the use of *white* to describe the
coats of the attendants who bring Bessie's body into the
courtroom highlights the insensitivity and moral depravity
that characterize the Daltons and Buckley, representative
characters of the white world. For Bessie's body, mutilated
and many days old, ironically becomes State's evidence to
prove that Bigger raped Mary Dalton. Inextricably related to
the ubiquitous snow and Mrs. Dalton's "white blur," these
more elusive references reflect the totality of whiteness in
the novel.

Of course, the metaphorical uses of *black* and *white* share
a dependent relationship: The fear and disgrace Bigger feels
about his blackness are enhanced by the cruelty and lack of
perceptivity he encounters in the white world. Conse-
quently, in some passages the words *black* and *white* appear
in the same line, punctuating the interrelationship between
Bigger's fear and the cause of his fear. Acquiring symbolic
dimensions, *black* and *white* coupled together represent Bigger's physical and emotional entrapment as well as the dehumanizing attitude that characterizes most of the novel's
white figures. Describing Bigger as he looks at a newspaper
when trying to escape, Wright explains, "He looked at the
paper and saw a black-and-white map of the South Side,
around the borders of which was a shaded portion an inch
deep." And later, after Bigger's confinement, the lines which
describe Buckley—the supreme representative of that white
world which dehumanizes Bigger—suggest Bigger's entrapment. As Buckley addresses the judge, "a white silk handkerchief peeped from the breast pocket of his black coat."
Very unfamiliar with the luxuries of a silk handkerchief,

Bigger has lived within the "shaded portion" of the map all his life, bound by the restrictions of Buckley's world. Emphasized by *white* and *black*, the effects of these restrictions on society culminate in the murder scene, for Mary Dalton's blind goodness and her insensitivity are as responsible for her death as is Bigger's fear.

A SUMMARY OF WRIGHT'S CRAFT

Because *Native Son*'s primary purpose is to delineate the emotional effects of the environment on Bigger's psyche, Wright chooses as his vehicle a novel of ideas in which the rhetorical functions of words and entire sentences coalesce as integral embodiments of this single purpose. A traditional examination of these minute stylistic aspects that characterize *Native Son* proves Wright to be a scrupulous craftsman. Through the function of alliteration, sound becomes an integral part of narrative action, subtly communicating the feelings of movement, anxiety, and fear. The sibilant *s*, particularly in the rat scene, functions as an agent that intensifies the chaos of the scene. Enhancing the novel's emotional impact, the periodic and balanced sentences summarize Bigger's thoughts and actions. Accompanying Wright's use of the compound sentence to punctuate the physical and emotional aberrations of a racial society is the symbolic use of the words *black* and *white*. Because scholars obsessively approach Wright's novel thematically, they have overlooked these distinctive qualities of his style.

The American Black Man's Experience Is Reflected Through Imagery in *Native Son*

James A. Emanuel

New York City College English professor James A. Emanuel is the author of a study of Langston Hughes and *The Treehouse*, a collection of poems. Here, Emanuel discusses how Wright employs concrete images (often terrifying ones) in *Native Son* which help readers understand not only Bigger Thomas and his feelings about himself, but also many other black men in America. Through a network of images, Emanuel writes, Wright illuminates the personal, racial, and national significance of the daily frustrations of African American life in his day.

The phrase "protest literature," no matter what adjectives surround it, reveals almost nothing of the permanent virtues of *Native Son*—although those virtues are profoundly anchored in blackness, in racial oppression, and in the militant spirit of the author. *Native Son* is a novel of remarkable agony, individualized in Bigger Thomas, yet universalized in ways grievously recognizable over a quarter of a century later, on almost every page, by Negro readers especially.

The question of how the author transmitted such power and truth should have been perfectly answered by now. To observe that Wright suffered keenly from racism and wrote feelingly about his experiences is merely to repeat what might equally be said of many black writers. Wright's racial fire is widely known, and it has long warmed a race in need of strong voices. The still challenging question, however, is literary: by what verbal techniques did the author help Bigger Thomas make the reader peep through his "knot-hole in

Excerpted from "Fever and Feeling: Notes on Imagery in *Native Son*," by James A. Emanuel, *Negro Digest*, vol. 18, no. 2, 1968. Reprinted with permission from the Johnson Publishing Co.

the fence" and understand his feelings about his existence? Bigger did not want to die without being understood by somebody. And Richard Wright has bequeathed one large means of understanding each Bigger Thomas among us, the very thing that Bigger hungered for after his capture: that "vast configuration of images and symbols whose magic and power could lift him up and make him live so intensely that the dread of being black and unequal would be forgotten . . ."

It is more than aestheticism that argues the value of images and symbols in Bigger's life. Largely existential in his perceptions, Bigger knows himself and his environment most surely through images. When despairing, he sees his life as "an obscene joke happening amid a colossal din of siren screams and white faces and circling lances of light under a cold and silken sky." When Bigger is walking with Bessie, his "*mind* could *feel* the soft swing of her body." A young man "consumed always with a body hunger," sensitive Bigger is vulnerable even to a ray of sunshine: in his cell near the end of the novel, a "shaft of yellow sun cut across his chest with as much weight as a beam forged of lead. With a convulsive gasp, he bent forward and shut his eyes." He yearns for wholeness of experience—made possible only when his feelings merge with some equivalent object around him—a yearning graphically portrayed when, lying on his cot in jail, Bigger's "hands were groping fumblingly through the city of men for something to match the feelings smoldering in him. . . ." Viewed internally as a conflict of forces, he is physically a centrally expanding "impulse always throbbing" but seldom countered by anything "outside of him to meet it and explain it." The symbolic cast of Bigger's mind is often made clear; for example, while he hides in an empty building, a chunk of bread in his pocket and his gun nestled under his shirt against his chest are described as symbolic of his rejection of folk religion. Bigger's tragedy, his abortive "sense of power, a power born of a latent capacity to live," is made palpable to the reader primarily through the sharing of his many "images charged with terror."

Native Son, then, enables the reader to live with a black "man of feeling" in the truest sense of the phrase, a young American whose specific ambition is "to merge himself with others and be a part of this world, to lose himself in it so he could find himself, to be allowed a chance to live like others, even though he was black." The constant frustration of that simple ambition and of the feelings supporting it is the psychological substance of the novel. The network of images that most authentically attend that daily frustration—and their personal, racial, and national significance—is the Jamesian "stuff of consciousness" to be conveyed.

A few miscellaneous techniques serving that end might be briefly mentioned. Images of light and dark, as expected, recur frequently, without special emphasis. The light in the Dalton house is hardly ever natural: it is a bright flood in the kitchen (a room important in racial history), is dim elsewhere in the home, and is hallucinatory and glaring in the semihuman furnace. Images of snow often suggest Bigger's complex connections—including aesthetic ones—with the "white world." When he leaps from the Daltons' window after the discovery of Mary's bones, for example, the "shock of [his fall] went through him, up his back to his head and he lay buried in a cold pile of snow, dazed. Snow was in his mouth, eyes, ears; snow was seeping down his back." A related type of imagery, temperature contrasts (such as Bigger's despairing wonder about the "warm red blood here and cold blue sky there)," marks the protagonist's awareness of paradox in his surroundings. Natural images of those surroundings used for the sake of sensory appeal unrelated to Bigger's mood of the moment occur fewer than five times in the whole novel. Other images of nature are even more rarely thematic; and the exception is interesting: after Bessie's murder, Bigger "lifted her, feeling the wind screaming a protest against him." Finally, what might be called "intestinal imagery" is skillfully used: the repeated image of Mary's severed head, urgent in Bigger's feelings rather than merely sensational on the page, catches fully the ambivalence and sensory horror that drive him. Similarly effective are pictures of the demonic furnace, with its "muffled breathing of the fire."

THE FURNACE

The furnace, emphatically described about 10 times, stands in the middle range of key images found in *Native Son*. That almost living, demanding-to-be-fed gorge whispers and sucks in its air (as Bigger sucks in air during his many moments of fearful tension). And no air can "get through" the furnace while Bigger stands breathless before the imminent discovery of Mary's bones, her earring, and the hatchet blade.

The full identification of the furnace activities with Bigger's own bodily sensations was incipient earlier when he neared collapse after sticking his ransom note under the Daltons' door: "A wave of numbness spread fanwise from his stomach over his entire body . . . making his mouth gap." Here the furnace mouth that Bigger has often peeked anxiously into becomes his own mouth, and the fan-shaped grate of glowing coals becomes his burning stomach. Later, as the incredulous newsman pokes at the bones in the furnace ashes, "[Bigger] himself was a huge furnace now through which no air could go; and the fear that surged into his stomach . . . was like the fumes of smoke that had belched from the ash bin." And as Bigger runs from the house, "the inside of his stomach glowed white-hot." The identification persists as Bigger notices newspaper headlines while walking to Bessie's room, resenting the failure of newsmen to take any interest in "*his* story"—meaning his very life—"as long as it had remained buried and burning in his own heart."

BIGGER'S NEED FOR SPACE

A rather peculiar image . . . occurs slightly more often than that of the furnace: the picture of an excited Bigger standing "in the middle of the floor." He leaps to this position at Bessie's when he wonders if he can trust her and when he wonders if the police are questioning his family at that very moment. He takes the same stance in his own room when he discovers that he has forgotten to burn his incriminating gloves, pencil, and paper; and he moves to the center of his jail cell when he is excited about the revelations of his first long talk with his lawyer, Max, and, again minutes later, when he first tries "to see himself in relation to other men." The meaning of these postures is specified when Bigger, fearfully embarrassed by the addition of his servile family and friends to the ranks of staring white people (the whole cast of the novel) already standing in his cell, "was so tense in body and mind that when the door swung in he bounded up and stood in the middle of the room." This peculiar image, then, pictorially frames some of Bigger's moments of maximum tension and freezes him at the point of maximum flight within areas that restrict his movement or thought. Daily trapped in corners and pockets on Chicago's South Side, at crucial instants Bigger needs space—at least that semblance of it represented by equidistance and centrality.

THE CROSS

A subtler geometric pattern . . . emerges when Bigger appears at the center of another figure, the Christian cross. At the inquest, with one policeman on each side of him and with two in front and two behind (totaling six, and therefore matching the number of jurors), Bigger moves ironically at the center of a cross. Afterwards, speeding through the streets toward the Dalton home for a bullying interrogation, Bigger rides with one officer seated on each side of him and with six police cars in front and a similar string behind, carried thus is the middle of an elongated crucifix (realistically adjusted to the spatial restrictions of traffic). While Bigger is resisting in the Dalton home the imposition of a false charge of rape, he confuses a cross being burned atop a building on the other side of the street with the cross recently hung around his neck by his mother's minister, Reverend Hammond. Thinking that a holy cross should not be burned, but hearing outside the cries "Burn 'im!" and "Kill 'im!," Bigger suddenly knows that he is not looking at "the cross of Christ, but the cross of the Ku Klux Klan. He had a cross of salvation round his throat and they were burning one to tell him that they hated him." Just as his body had metaphorically become the furnace, it becomes the cross when a jailer attributes his rebellion against the religious symbol to Communist dogma: "'That's a goddamn lie!' Bigger shouted. His body seemed a flaming cross as words boiled hysterically out of him." After Bigger throws his cross away three times, the author's condensed metaphor shows the meaning of these several pages in Book Three: Bigger reflects that "the cross the preacher had hung round his throat had been burned in front of his eyes."

BLINDNESS

Wright takes pains with less noticeable images. Such is the case with his depiction of eyes as emblems of blindness and guilt (exclusive of his many pictures of the blind Mrs. Dalton). Strangely liberated by his accidental murder of Mary, Bigger thinks about nearby people waiting for street cars:

> He did not look at them; they were simply blind people, blind like his mother, his brother, his sister, Peggy, Britten, Jan, Mr. Dalton, and the sightless Mrs. Dalton and the quiet empty houses with their black gaping windows.

Those "blind" houses in the ghetto, according to Bigger's

feelings, have stares like that of the Dalton's white cat that leaped upon his shoulder in front of photographers in the basement when Mary's bones were discovered, "its big round black eyes twin pools of secret guilt," and like that of the murdered Bessie, "staring at him with those round large black eyes, her bloody mouth open in awe and wonder and pain. . . ." To a person like Bigger, his life reduced to occasional sensory joys snuffed out by a constant overbalance of pain, images of the corruption of the eye—his only receptor of magnitude—would disturbingly crowd his mind.

BLOTTING OUT

Two kinds of images are thematically as well as numerically impressive in *Native Son*, each found in various passages between fifteen and twenty times. The type discernible slightly less often, the "blot-out" image, shares the powers of physical violence upon its initial appearance, the day Bigger first comes to 4605 Drexel Boulevard and wants "to wave his hand and blot out" Mr. Dalton for making him feel embarrassed, or, failing in that, "to blot himself out." Using the same or quite similar words, Bigger wants to "blot out" a number of people and things before the novel ends. This list of people includes Negroes because they never act in unity, catching "the mind and body in certainty and faith"; whites because they are "measuring every inch of his weakness"; and all the people at the inquest because they look at and cause him to look at Bessie's corpse. But Bigger's destructive impulse as made known through this kind of image is usually aimed elsewhere. It is aimed, for example, at inactivity: planning the ransom note, he does not "need to dance and sing and clown over the floor in order to blot out a day and night of doing nothing." It is aimed at sound, blotted out by the "roaring noise in his ears," for instance, when he hates Britten "so hard and hot" for being a bigot; at fear, "blotted out" by his sudden confidence when he eats breakfast with his family and thinks of "how blind they were"; and at death itself, "a different and bigger adversary" than "the white mountain" of vengeful society.

In a reversal of this variety of imagery, white society itself becomes an arbitrary agent of the blotting-out impulse surrounding Bigger, for it feels "that nothing short of a quick blotting out of his life would make the city safe again." All of society colludes in such destruction, points out Max: "Your

Honor, injustice blots out one form of life, but another grows up in its place with its own rights, needs, and aspirations." Max himself, however, his hat "jammed" on his head in that subtle last scene of the novel, has in effect blotted out of his head all the words from Bigger that he did not want to hear, those expressions of the black prisoner's superior humanity that outdistanced Communist dogma.

THE WHITE BLUR

The other kind of image thematic in *Native Son* with about equal frequency is the "white blur" and its variant forms. Bigger's certainty of the color and his uncertainty regarding the substance of these sense impressions invest them with a degree of pathos and irony. Blind Mrs. Dalton, always dressed in white, both a victim and an object of faulty external perception, is typically a "white blur . . . standing by the door, silent, ghostlike." Other people pictorially share her color and meaning: while Bigger stands bewildered by his discovery that he has killed Mary, a "vast city of white people" blurs the reality of the room; while viewing his picture in the newspaper, in which the white cat perches accusingly on his shoulder, Bigger feels that the "whole vague white world . . . would track him down . . ."; and while he is being cruelly dragged and cursed and stamped in the snow, he dimly sees around him "an array of faces, white and looming." An implicit image of the "white blur"—and a source of monumental frustration in Bigger Thomas and in many of his progeny—is voiced by Max, who tells the judge that the prisoner "had no notion before he murdered, and he has none now, of having been wronged by any specific individuals." Material objects in the "white world" also appear as blurs. The reader slowly realizes that the white-owned cars that "whirred over the smooth black asphalt," "shot past them at high speed," and "zoomed past on swift rubber tires" early in the novel have been varicolored forerunners of the white blur. When images like "the white flash of a dozen silver bulbs" occur, the mass image of the newsmen in the basement has a manifold significance.

A reversal like that observed in the blot-out images appears in the use of the white blur. State's Attorney Buckley, himself part of the white blur, urges the death penalty to enable whites "to sleep in peace tonight, to know that tomorrow will not bring the black shadow of death over the

homes and lives." The sentence of death brings another reversal, a counter image, to Bigger's perception as he understands "every word" while reacting only to "the judge's
white face, his eyes not blinking." The "blur" now disappears from the language of the novel, clarified by its own revealed deadliness—to recur implicitly and indirectly only
once, transformed into a "new adversary" for Bigger: the
opaqueness in the mind of Max that blurs his "deeper
awareness" of his client.

THE WALL AND CURTAIN

By far the most numerous and the most meaningful,
Wright's closely related images of the wall and the curtain,
widely distributed in over fifty separate passages in *Native
Son*, deserve a closer study than is possible here. But their
categories (thirteen in number), at least, can be indicated.
When ranked according to frequency of usage, the wall-
curtain as a shield of indifference and detachment, emphasized in eleven different passages, is predominant. On the
first morning of the novel, Bigger has "lurked behind his
curtain of indifference . . . snapping and glaring at whatever
had tried to make him come out into the open." Several such
images cluster on the pages describing Bigger's capture,
where the reader sees him trapped on the icy water tank,
"going behind his curtain, his wall, looking out with sullen
stares of contempt"; "behind his curtain now, looking down
at himself freezing under the impact of water in sub-zero
winds"; and when his fingers are too stiff to pick up his gun,
"Something laughed in him, cold and hard; he was laughing
at himself." The final such image in the novel is especially
interesting: "Bigger's eyes were wide and unseeing; his voice
rushed on" as he explains to Max important things about his
life and recent actions that Max really does not want to hear.
Bigger is walling Max out of his perceptions, so that he, Bigger, can better gauge with his feelings whether his own *tone*
is carrying his meaning (it had been Max's tone in court, not
his words, that had made him believe "that Max knew how
he felt").

A category of wall-curtain images used somewhat less often, and used negatively, is one reflecting on the artificial
separation of certain classes of people: Bigger, for example,
rides in the front seat of the Dalton car "between two vast
white looming walls [Mary and Jan]." The suggestion of pro-

tectiveness in this kind of image disappears from the novel after white but "honest" Jan has approached Bigger, "flung aside the curtain and walked into the room of his life"—a passage important also for its metaphor showing Bigger's life as a room, and therefore enhancing the meaning of every wall-curtain image. Thus reversed, the image later pictures Bigger trying to break down walls to reach other people. One of the most gratifying passages in the novel employs such an image when the prisoner wonders whether, if his hands were electric wires and his heart a battery, and if he

> reached out through these stone walls and felt other hands
> . . . would there be a reply, a shock? Not that he wanted those
> hearts to turn their warmth to him; . . . But just to know that
> they were there and warm! . . . And in that touch, response of
> recognition, there would be union, identity; . . . a wholeness
> which had been denied him all his life.

Similarly moved by his new insight, Bigger wonders how he can "break down this wall of isolation" between him and Max, whom he now sees "upon another planet, far off in space"; and he apprehensively tells Max that maybe the wall between him and other men will still be there when he is executed: "I'll be feeling and thinking that they didn't see me and I didn't see them"—an early expression of Ralph Ellison's "invisible man" theme.

The remaining 11 subdivisions of the wall-curtain image, spread throughout approximately 35 passages, need not be illustrated by more excerpts to document the variety and authenticity in this area of Wright's style. Nevertheless, the following list of the subdivisions, ranked again according to their frequency of use, should be informative. The other figurative walls and curtains, then, vividly represent (1) the suppression of certain feelings; (2) hatred, resentment, and mistrust; (3) the stunting or perversions of intelligence and imagination; (4) the withering of familial and friendly affection; (5) the ineffectiveness of certain barriers; (6) the deprivation of fundamental human needs; (7) natural barriers; (8) entrapment; (9) deceit; (10) defensive counterfeelings; and (11) the acceptance of certain isolation.

A knowledge of all the images in *Native Son* does not produce automatically a knowledge of Bigger Thomas. And Bigger himself feels more than he thinks, concluding at last, existentially, that his feelings are the surest guide to truth and to morality. "But when I think of why all the killing was," he says (apparently including all the fancied killings of his life), "I begin to feel what I wanted, what I am." To know what and why a man desires, and to know what he is, is the deepest human engagement of our faculties. The furnace, the trembling poise in the middle of the room, the crucifix, the haunting blind eyes, the wish to blot out, the "white blur" of the hater and avenger, and the looming wall so massively effective and yet so useless and wrong—all these images metaphorically dramatize part of the black man's American experience; and *Native Son* preserves them for us to feel and to believe.

The Violence of the Beast: Animal Imagery in *Native Son*

Robert Felgar

Robert Felgar, associate professor of English at Jacksonville State University, Alabama, examines Wright's use of often violent animal imagery in *Native Son*. Blacks are referred to as pigs, gorillas, and other animals by whites in the novel who do not realize, Felgar writes, that they share the blame for Bigger's violence. The Daltons' white cat, a symbol of white guilt and hostility, watches over Bigger as he becomes a "beast," killing to survive in the ghetto like any animal in the jungle.

When Buckley, the State's Attorney in *Native Son*, sums up the prosecution's case, he says, "Man stepped forward from the kingdom of the beast the moment he felt that he could think and feel in security, knowing that sacred law had taken the place of his gun and knife." In making the statement, Buckley unknowingly and ironically described from the white point of view the world of Bigger Thomas and of America, because Bigger is a beast among beasts, living in the wild forest. The discursive narrative line in the novel is developed, commented upon, and reinforced by Wright's use of images from man's primitive original state, which, as Wright shows, still obtains in the white man's view of the black man's world.

The pattern of beast imagery informs the violent opening scene in which Bigger and his family awake to the sound of "a light tapping in the thinly plastered walls of the room." A huge black rat finds itself trapped in the Thomas's one-room apartment: "The rat squeaked and turned and ran in a narrow circle, looking for a place to hide; it leaped again past Bigger. . . . The rat's belly pulsed with fear. Bigger advanced a

Excerpted from "'The Kingdom of the Beast': The Landscape of *Native Son*," by Robert Felgar, *College Language Association Journal*, vol. 17, 1974. Reprinted by permission of the *College Language Association Journal*.

step and the rat emitted a long thin song of defiance, its black beady eyes glittering, its tiny forefeet pawing the air restlessly." Bigger throws a skillet at the rat and then smashes its head with a shoe, which not only helps to establish the violent prospect of *Native Son* but also functions structurally in that the scene forestalls what Bigger will later do to Bessie and what will later happen to Bigger himself: he will be a black rat in the white man's world, running and looking desperately for a hole to crawl into. The rat is also used expressionistically to objectify Bigger's own inner fear and fury at finding himself trapped in a white world with no escape.

As in the oppressor's stereotype, the Thomas family "lives like pigs." Like a frightened animal, Bigger "lurked behind his curtain of indifference and looked at things, snapping and glaring at whatever had tried to make him come out into the open." The cinema reflects the same stereotypical image of the black man: Jack and Bigger decide to go to the Regal to see *The Gay Woman* and *Trader Horn;* the latter "was shown on the posters in terms of black men and black women dancing against a wild background of barbaric jungle." To Bigger's remark that he would like to go to the white nightclub in *The Gay Woman,* Jack replies, "Man, if them folks saw you they'd run. . . . They'd think a gorilla broke loose from the zoo and put on a tuxedo." Buckley and the frenzied white mob refer to Bigger repeatedly as a "black ape." Wright has given his white readers one of their own projections—the black man as a murderous, depraved beast; what most of the white characters in the book fail to realize, of course, is that they are more monstrous than Bigger because they share the ultimate responsibility for his being able to create and possess himself only through animal violence, only through cunning and fierceness.

THE WHITE CAT

The fearsome black rat in Bigger's own home finds its imagistic counterpart in the Dalton mansion in Kate, the ubiquitous white cat. When Mrs. Dalton walks down her hallway after briefly meeting her new chauffeur, "a big white cat, pacing without sound," follows her; it looks at Bigger "with large placid eyes." It is an intensified, animal image of the hostile white environment Bigger is in. Ironically, it is Mary, the liberal communist sympathizer and daughter to the Daltons, who picks up Kate and carries her out of the room in which Mr. Dalton is questioning Bigger. The feline symbol of white guilt and hostility even watches Bigger while he tries to dispose of Mary's corpse:

> A noise made him whirl; two green burning pools—pools of accusation and guilt—stared at him from a white blur that sat perched upon the edge of the trunk. His mouth opened in a silent scream and his body became hotly paralyzed. It was the white cat and its round green eyes gazed past him at the white face hanging limply from the fiery furnace door. *God!* He closed his mouth and swallowed. Should he catch the cat and kill it and put it in the furnace, too? He made a move. The cat stood up; its white fur bristled; its back arched. He tried to grab it and it bounded past him with a long wail of fear and scampered up the steps and through the door and out of sight. Oh! He had left the kitchen door open. *That* was it. He closed the door and stood again before the furnace, thinking, cats can't talk.

Bigger can never escape Kate and all she represents: hostility, exclusion, fear. Bigger is Kate's prey; she will never give up the chase. While the newspaper reporters question Mr. Dalton about his missing daughter, Kate "leaped with one movement upon Bigger's shoulder and sat perched there. . . . He tried to lift the cat down; but its claws clutched his coat." The white beast has caught Bigger and will devour him. Later, in Bigger's picture in the newspaper, Kate sits perched on his shoulder.

THE ANIMAL LANDSCAPE

The contours of the second book, "Flight," are also largely determined by Wright's use of animal imagery. Widow Thomas remarks to her son, "You jumped like something bit you," when she sees him Sunday morning, after Mary has been smothered, decapitated, and placed in the Daltons' furnace, which is like a fire-breathing dragon whose horrible maw must be satisfied. Vera, Bigger's sister, sobs that her older brother makes her feel like a dog, while Buddy is described as being "like a chubby puppy," no match for the monsters of the encircling white world. Bigger characterizes Bessie, his girl, as a rabbit, always fearful and timid in the face of the possible consequences of fighting back against the white oppressor.

The black ghetto is the kingdom of the beast. Its streets are "long paths leading through a dense jungle, lit here and there with torches held high in invisible hands." Staying in the old abandoned houses while hiding from the beast will be like "hiding in a jungle," Bigger says. The old houses are rat-infested and dangerous. In the chase, Bigger corresponds to the fox or the hare, the members of the white police to hounds; there is never any doubt that, like the rat in the opening scene, the native son will be caught and killed, and Bigger knows it: "this whole vague white world . . . was more than a match for him . . . soon it would track him down and have it out with him." Finally about to be caught, Bigger hides from the beast on top of a water tank, but it uses a powerful jet of water to force him off: "The icy water clutched again at his body like a giant hand; the chill of it squeezed him like the circling coils of a monstrous boa constrictor." To literalize the metaphor, the prey is being suffocated in the jungle. Later, at the inquest, Bigger wishes he had cheated the beast out of "this hunt, this eager sport" by letting it kill him.

BIGGER AS BEAST

In "Fate," the third and last book of *Native Son,* Wright draws continually upon the source of his basic, informing metaphor, the kingdom of the beast. The eponymous hero begins to accept it himself: "Maybe they were right when they said that a black skin was bad, the covering of an apelike animal." The white newspapers exploit the metaphor relentlessly:

> He looks exactly like an ape!' exclaimed a terrified young white girl. . . . His lower jaw protrudes obnoxiously, reminding one of a jungle beast. . . . All in all, he seems a beast utterly untouched by the softening influences of modern civilization. . . . He acted like an earlier missing link in the human species. He seemed out of place in a white man's civilization.

Max, Bigger's communist attorney, points out the metaphor to the jury, but they are blind, like everyone else in the novel:

> It [the corpse of black people] has made itself a home in the wild forest of our great cities, amid the rank and choking vegetation of slums! . . . In order to live it has sharpened its claws! . . . By night it creeps from its lair and steals toward the settlements of civilization! And at the sight of a kind face it does not lie down upon its back and kick up its heels playfully to be tickled and stroked. No; it leaps to kill!

Buckley uses the same imagery in his summing up speech, only he does not realize or will not publically admit that men like him have made Bigger into a monster; he warns the court against other "half-human black ape[s]" and refers to

Bigger as "a bestial monstrosity," a "black lizard . . . scuttling on his belly . . . over the earth and spitting forth his venom of death!" Later he calls him a "black mad dog," a "rapacious beast," a "black cur," a "maddened ape," an "infernal monster," a "treacherous beast," a "coiled rattler," a "worthless ape," a "demented savage." It is of course the height of irony that Buckley should call Bigger names far more applicable to Buckley himself.

Pervasive throughout *Native Son* is imagery from the kingdom of the beast. Bigger is a "nigger," a black ape, a tiger stalking its white prey, as the stereotypical white racist notion has it. But in the wild forest no other way exists for him to find himself and give himself some status, but violence, the law of the jungle. To survive in such a world, one must be a cunning and fierce animal, for obeying the law will only exact one's humanity as the price for submission. To be free, one must, like a beast in the jungle, kill before one is killed. In the kingdom of the beast the only law is self-preservation. The kingdom of the beast revolves around violence and is Wright's objective correlative for, his objectification of, whites' inner stereotypical vision of the black world. The prospect of *Native Son* is a wild forest in which beast preys upon beast.

Wright's Allusions to Color-Blindness in *Native Son*

Seymour L. Gross

Wright scholar Seymour L. Gross of the University of Detroit focuses on the three Dalton characters of *Native Son* as symbols of blindness (being blind to or blinded by color) in the novel. Mrs. Dalton is literally blind, Mr. Dalton is blind to the fact that Bigger comes from the slum tenement he owns, and Mary Dalton is blinded by her own good intentions. Additionally, Gross suggests that Wright knew the history of John Dalton, the man who discovered "color-blindness," when choosing the name Dalton for his characters.

Much of the . . . criticism of Richard Wright's *Native Son* (1940) has turned attention to the symbolic texture of the novel in an attempt to locate the artistic sources of its social passion and, at least implicitly, to cast doubt on the charge that it is another example of a sociological novel in which everything is taken seriously but the writing. One result of these efforts has been to show us how carefully Wright utilizes a pattern of sight and blindness imagery to expose the agonizing permutations of color in America. Every major figure in the novel, with the exception of Bigger, and he only at the verge of death, is either blind to or blinded by color. There are those who cannot (or will not) see how utterly decisive color has been in America and so go on mistakenly acting in terms of the "colorless" images thrown up on the screen of their hopeful politics or compensatory religion or fantasies of "playing white." For others, the vast majority, pigmentation is so visually imperative that they are blind to everything but the shapes projected by their preconditioned moral view of color.

The distortion of vision (that is, perception) is interest-

Excerpted from "'Dalton' and Color-Blindness in *Native Son*," by Seymour L. Gross, *Mississippi Quarterly*, vol. 27, 1973–74. Reprinted with permission from Mississippi State University.

ingly explored in the three Daltons. Mrs. Dalton is literally blind and so cannot see Bigger at all; indeed, it is because she cannot see what is really going on in the bedroom (Bigger is merely putting the intoxicated Mary to bed) that Bigger is driven to kill Mary. Bigger knows that in the inner eye of America a black man in a white woman's bedroom is already a "nigger rapist." Mr. Henry Dalton is so blind that he cannot see that the "boy" whom he has given a chance to make something of himself but who kills his daughter is the same color as the occupants of his over-priced slum dwellings. And Mary Dalton is so blind to what color has made of Bigger that she disastrously treats him as if he were already the liberated embodiment of her good intentions.

THE REAL DALTON

In view of such a symbolic pattern, the name Wright chose to give his white family takes on appreciable significance, for it was John Dalton who in 1794 first gave an account of the optical distortion thenceforth to be known as Daltonism, or color-blindness. Indeed, the title of Dalton's paper, "Extraordinary Facts Relating to the Vision of Colors," could serve as the epigraph to *Native Son*. But is the name which so beautifully encapsulates the two dominant strains in the novel—color and blindness—evidence of Wright's self-conscious artistry or is it merely a remarkable coincidence?

Did Wright know that Daltonism is color-blindness? After all, it is not a fact known to every schoolboy; nor is it such an unusual name that coincidence is immediately ruled out. Wright's biographer, Constance Webb, points out, for example, that Dalton was the name of a street near where Wright had lived in Jackson, Mississippi. Moreover, if Wright wanted to establish a connection between the discoverer of color-blindness and his fictional family, why then did he name the father Henry rather than John?

Circumstantially speaking, Wright was a far better bet to know about Daltonism than the average non-medical man. Frederic Wertham, Wright's psychiatrist-friend, believes that Wright learned the meaning of the term when he was working as a medical orderly in Chicago in 1932, which is of course quite possible. But he could also have learned about it while working for a Memphis optical company before he came north. He was interested enough in the optical business to consider making it his life's work. Further, Wright, like most autodidacts, had an unusual abundance of miscellaneous information in many fields, including medicine. One of his adolescent dreams, Webb tells us, was to become a researcher in a medical laboratory. On one occasion when Wright's friend Horace Cayton had a tooth pulled, Wright launched into an anatomical description of the nerve endings of teeth. When Cayton asked him how he knew such things, Wright replied that he had read a book on dentistry and then proceeded "to describe the functions of the body." "'Anybody can be a doctor,' Wright announced. 'You just sit down and read.'"

The reason for Wright's having chosen to call his Dalton Henry rather than John can perhaps be explained by the 1939 Chicago telephone directory. Of the 103 Daltons listed, there are nine John Daltons but no Henry Daltons (most of the other common given male names are also represented). Considering the nature of the portrait of Mr. Dalton in *Native Son*, to have named him John could have turned each of the nine real John Daltons into possible litigants, or at least bothers.

Since Wright never outrightly admitted the symbolic use of the Dalton name, the evidence presented here for believing that he did so is admittedly speculative. But until such time as the negative view of the matter is absolutely established, it does not strike me as unreasonable to believe that Wright's use of the Dalton name was more than a coincidence.

The Conclusion of *Native Son* Is Often Misunderstood

Paul N. Siegel

Literary scholar Paul N. Siegel of Long Island University in New York takes issue with other critics' claims that *Native Son* is flawed because the conclusion of the novel, and Max's courtroom speech in particular, relies on Communist Party rhetoric. Siegel suggests, however, that Max does not speak for the Communist Party and in fact becomes a positive force in the book, calling for an end of hatred and repression in America. Likewise, although reviewers have criticized Wright for what they see as Bigger Thomas's defeat, Siegel maintains that Bigger experiences a kind of victory, finding freedom and self-acceptance in his acts of violence and subsequent death sentence.

The conclusion of *Native Son* has perhaps caused more critics, distinguished and obscure, to go astray, reading into it their own preconceptions instead of perceiving the author's purpose, than any other significant portion of a major work of modern American literature. Both Max's lengthy speech in the courtroom and his final scene with Bigger have been grievously misunderstood.

Let us turn to Irving Howe as our prime example:

> The long speech by Bigger's radical lawyer Max . . . is ill-related to the book itself: Wright had not achieved Dreiser's capacity for absorbing everything, even the most recalcitrant philosophical passages, into a unified vision of things. . . . Yet it should be said that the endlessly-repeated criticism that Wright caps his melodrama with a party-line oration tends to oversimplify the novel, for Wright is too honest simply to allow the propagandistic message to constitute the last word. Indeed, the last word is given not to Max but to Bigger. For at the

Excerpted from "The Conclusion of Richard Wright's *Native Son*," by Paul N. Siegel, *PMLA*, vol. 89, 1974. Reprinted with permission from the Modern Language Association of America.

end Bigger remains at the mercy of his hatred and fear, the lawyer retreats helplessly, the projected union between political consciousness and raw revolt has not been achieved—as if Wright were persuaded that, all ideology apart, there is for each Negro an ultimate trial that he can bear only by himself.

Howe, therefore, finds that the "endlessly-repeated criticism" that Max's speech is a "party-line oration" "tends to oversimplify the novel" not because this criticism is incorrect but because it does not go beyond the speech to perceive that the union of Bigger's "raw revolt" and Max's "political consciousness" has not been effected. So, too, Alfred Kazin declares that Wright's method is "to astonish the reader by torrential scenes of cruelty, hunger, rape, murder and flight, and then enlighten him by crude Stalinist homilies." By "crude Stalinist homilies" Kazin undoubtedly means Max's speech and his conversations with Bigger.

Howe, Kazin, . . . and numerous other critics . . . have responded to the courtroom speech with a conditioned reflex: Richard Wright was a Communist; Boris Max is called a Communist (only, to be sure, by the red-baiting prosecuting attorney and newspapers, but that is overlooked); therefore, the speech must be a "party-line oration," a "crude Stalinist" homily. Before we examine the speech, let us see what Ben Davis, Jr., a leading black official of the Communist party at the time, had to say about it in reviewing the book in the *Sunday Worker,* the official organ of the party.

MAX DOES NOT SPEAK FOR THE COMMUNIST PARTY

Although Davis concedes that "certain passages in Max's speech show an understanding of the responsibility of capitalism for Bigger's plight," he checks off the following points against Max: "he accepts the idea that Negroes have a criminal psychology"; "he does not challenge the false charge of rape against Bigger"; "he does not deal with the heinous murder of Bessie, tending to accept the bourbon policy that crimes of Negroes against each other don't matter"; "he argues that Bigger, and by implication the whole Negro mass, should be held in jail to protect 'white daughters'"; he "should have argued for Bigger's acquittal in the case, and should have helped stir the political pressure of the Negro and white masses to get that acquittal." "His speech," Davis concludes, ". . . expresses the point of view held . . . by . . . reformist betrayers. . . . The first business of the Communist Party or of the

I.L.D. would have been to chuck him out of the case."

Whatever the distortions in the pronouncement of this party bureaucrat turned literary critic, he is, it must be acknowledged, a more authoritative interpreter of the party line of the time than either Howe or Kazin. Davis obviously wants the simplified propaganda that *Native Son* does not give: a hero who is a completely innocent victim and a lawyer who thunders his client's innocence, who brilliantly exposes a frame-up rooted in a corrupt society, and who calls for giant demonstrations against this frame-up. The fact that Max is not a party-line expounder is one of the points that made the party leaders uneasy about *Native Son,* an uneasiness indicated by the review itself and by the fact that Davis' review appeared a month after the novel's publication.

The novel itself indicates that Max is not a Communist party member. Jan tells Mary that Max is "one of the best lawyers we've got." He does not refer to him as a "comrade," a member of the Communist party, but as one of the lawyers employed by the International Labor Defense, the legal defense organization controlled by the party. Although Max is obviously sympathetic to the causes espoused by the Communists, the fact that he is employed by the International Labor Defense does not indicate that he is a Communist any more than the employment of the noted criminal lawyer Samuel S. Leibowitz in the Scottsboro case meant that Leibowitz was a Communist. When he tells Bigger that others besides blacks are hated, he says, "They hate trade unions. They hate folks who try to organize. They hate Jan." "They hate Jan"—not "Communists like me and Jan." Later he says, "I'm a Jew and they hate me"—not "I'm a Communist and a Jew and they hate me."

If, then, Max is not the novel's Communist spokesman who delivers a "party-line oration," what are his politics and what does he say in his speech? An old, wise, weary Jew, deeply aware of the radical defects of the society of which he is a member, Max, as we shall see in his courtroom speech, envisions a cataclysmic end to this society and seeks desperately to avert it by striving to have wrongs redressed. He is neither a revolutionist nor a Stalinist.

MAX CALLS FOR AN END OF HATRED AND REPRESSION

His speech is not an address to a jury, as Edwin Berry Burgum, James Baldwin, Dan McCall, and Edward Margolies

affirm. Max clearly states that, not daring to put Bigger's fate
in the hands of a white jury whose minds have been in-
flamed by the press, he has entered a plea of guilty, which
by the laws of Illinois permits him to reject a trial by jury
and to have the sentence rendered by the presiding judge.
"Dare I," he asks the judge, " . . . put his fate in the hands of
a jury . . . whose minds are already conditioned by the press
of the nation. . . ? No! I could not! So today I come to face this
Court, rejecting a trial by jury, willingly entering a plea of
guilty, asking in the light of the laws of this state that this
boy's life be spared."

It is to this judge that Max is speaking. Beyond the judge
he is speaking to "men of wealth and property," who, if they
misread "the consciousness of the submerged millions today," will bring about a civil war in the future. It is amazing
that James Baldwin can say that Max's speech "is addressed
to those among us of good will and it seems to say that,
though there are whites and blacks among us who hate each
other, we will not; there are those who are betrayed by greed,
by guilt, by blood, by blood lust, but not we; we will set our
faces against them and join hands and walk together into
that dazzling future when there will be no white or black."
Baldwin is here carried away by his own rhetoric. There is
not a sentence in the speech stating or implying a dazzling
future to which black and white will walk hand in hand!

Nor is the speech a savage attack on capitalism or a statement of a "guilt-of-the-nation thesis," a plea for sympathy for
one whose guilt we must all share. "Allow me, Your Honor,"
says Max, " . . . to state emphatically that I do *not* claim that
this boy is a victim of injustice, nor do I ask that this Court
be sympathetic with him. . . . If I should say that he is a victim of injustice, then I would be asking by implication for
sympathy; and if one insists upon looking at this boy in the
light of sympathy, he will be swamped by a feeling of guilt
so strong as to be indistinguishable from hate."

The mob of would-be lynchers, he says, knowing in its
heart of the oppression of Negroes, is as possessed of guilt,
fear, and hate as Bigger is. In order to understand the full
significance of Bigger's case, he urges the judge, one must
rise above such emotion. To do so, he summons him to look
upon it from a historical height. The "first wrong," the en-
slavement of the Negroes, was "understandable and inevitable," for in subduing this "harsh and wild country" men

had to use other men as tools and weapons. "Men do what they must do." From that first wrong came a sense of guilt, in the attempted stifling of which came hate and fear, a hate and fear that matched that of the Negroes. Injustice practiced on this scale and over that length of time "is injustice no longer; it is an accomplished fact of life." This fact of life is a system of oppression squeezing down upon millions of people. These millions can be stunted, but they cannot be stamped out. And as oppression grows tighter, guilt, fear, and hatred grow stronger on both sides. Killing Bigger will only "swell the tide of pent-up lava that will some day break loose, not in a single, blundering, accidental, individual crime, but in a wild cataract of emotion that will brook no control." Sentencing him to life imprisonment, on the other hand, will give him an opportunity to "build a meaning for his life."

Max's speech is, in short, an agonized plea to the judge to understand the significance of Bigger and, understanding, to break through the pattern of hatred and repression that "makes our future seem a looming image of violence." It has been frequently pointed out that in Book III, which is entitled "Fate," we see realized the doom of Bigger that has been foreshadowed from the beginning. This is entirely true, of course, but "Fate" also refers to the doom of the United States, toward which Max sees us, "like sleepwalkers," proceeding. "If we can understand how subtly and yet strongly his life and fate are linked to ours,—if we can do this, perhaps we shall find the key to our future." Bigger killed "accidentally"—that is, he was not aware of killing as he killed, but this does not matter. What matters is that "every thought he thinks is potential murder." "Who knows when another 'accident' involving millions of men will happen, an 'accident' that will be the dreadful day of our doom?"

Max's speech, far from being, as Howe says, "ill-related to the book," not a part of "a unified vision of things," grows out of the rest of the novel. It has, to be sure, a number of weaknesses. It and the prosecuting attorney's speech are not seen and heard from Bigger's point of view, which is otherwise rigidly adhered to in the novel, the vivid presentation of Bigger's visceral reactions, as events are registered on his consciousness, contributing to the novel's force and drive. Max's speech, which takes sixteen pages, is not, however, summarized and presented through Bigger's consciousness, and at its end we are told that Bigger "had not understood the speech, but he had felt the meaning of some of it from the tone of Max's voice." Moreover, the speech, far from being superimposed on what had gone on before and at variance with it, repeats too obviously what has already been said. Wright's awareness of this repetition and his desire to achieve a heightened effect in the final summing up may explain a rhetoric that is occasionally too highly wrought and too highly pitched.

MAX'S SPEECH REITERATES THEMES OF BLINDNESS

That the speech, however, is not an obtrusion is indicated by the number of recurring themes and images in the novel that the speech brings together. The first theme that we might consider is that of blindness. Bigger, eating his breakfast the morning after he has killed Mary and looking upon his family and the world with new eyes, realizes that his mother, sister, and brother exclude from their vision of the world that which they do not wish to see. He also realizes that Mrs. Dalton is blind figuratively as well as literally, that Mr. Dalton and Jan are blind, and that Mary had been blind in not recognizing that which was in him, the propensity to kill. When he joins Bessie, he feels the same about her being blind as he does about his family. She knows nothing but hard work in white folks' kitchens and the liquor she drinks to make up for her starved life. In flight, despite the danger of death, Bigger feels a "queer sense of power" at having set the chase in motion, at being engaged in purposeful activity for the first time in his life, and thinks, "He was living, truly and deeply, no matter what others might think, looking at him with their blind eyes." When Jan visits him in prison, he tells Bigger, "I was kind of blind. . . . I didn't know we were so far apart until that night." Bigger, understanding that Jan is expressing his belief in him, for the first time looks upon a white man as a human being. "He saw Jan as though someone had performed an operation upon his eyes."

Max, in his image of the American people proceeding to their doom like sleepwalkers, catches up these images of darkness present on all sides. It is this blindness that he emphasizes throughout his speech. If the judge reacts only to what he has to say about the sufferings of Negroes, he states, he will be "blinded" by a feeling that will prevent him from perceiving reality and acting accordingly. "Rather, I plead with you to see . . . an existence of men growing out of the soil prepared by the collective but blind will of a hundred million people." "Your Honor," he exclaims, "in our blindness we have so contrived and ordered the lives of men" that their every human aspiration constitutes a threat to the state.

Max, then, sees the American people as going unseeingly to their doom because they—except, presumably, for a possibly saving remnant of them such as Max himself and his co-workers—either actively support or passively and unthinkingly accept the institutions of a repressive society. Bigger for his part sees whites as constituting an overwhelming natural force, a part of the structure of the universe. "To Bigger and his kind," says Wright early in the novel, "white people were not really people; they were a sort of great natural force, like a stormy sky looming overhead, or like a deep swirling river stretching suddenly at one's feet in the dark." The snowstorm that covers Chicago after Bigger's murder is symbolic of the hostile white world. When Bigger slips in running, "the white world tilted at a sharp angle and the icy wind shot past his face." The snow separates Jan and Bigger from each other, as Jan accosts Bigger in the street after Mary's disappearance and tries to speak to him, only to be driven away by Bigger's gun: "In the pale yellow sheen of the street lamp they faced each other; huge wet flakes of snow floated down slowly, forming a delicate screen between them." When Jan gets through to Bigger in prison, an image of the white world as a great natural force is used again, this time a force subject to erosion: "Jan had spoken a declaration of friendship that would make other white men hate him: a particle of white rock had detached itself from that looming mountain of white hate and had rolled down the slope, stopping still at his feet."

With his fine sensitivity, Max understands Bigger's feeling about whites, which Bigger had conveyed to him in the prison interview, and tries to make the judge understand it, using the same image of the white world as a natural force, not made up of human beings: "When situations like this arise, instead of men feeling that they are facing other men, they feel that they are facing mountains, floods, seas." But the judge blindly does not understand.

BIGGER FINDS FREEDOM IN KILLING

Another recurring image is that of the wall or curtain or veil behind which Bigger withdraws and hides rather than face reality. "He knew that the moment he allowed himself to feel to its fullness how [his family] lived, the shame and misery of their lives, he would be swept out of himself with fear and despair. So he held toward them an attitude of iron reserve; he lived with them, but behind a wall, a curtain. And toward himself he was even more exacting. He knew that the moment he allowed what his life meant to enter fully into his consciousness, he would either kill himself or someone else." So, Max says, the killing of Mary was "a sudden and violent rent in the veil behind which he lived," tearing aside his alienated feelinglessness and enabling him for the first time really to live.

The theme that Bigger's killing has given him a freedom he never before had is sounded frequently. "He had murdered and created a new life for himself. It was something that was all his own, and it was the first time in his life he had had anything that others could not take from him." And again: "He felt that he had his destiny in his grasp. He was more alive than he could ever remember having been; his mind and attention were pointed, focussed toward a goal." And still again: "There remained to him a queer sense of power. *He* had done this. *He* had brought all this about. In all of his life these two murders were the most meaningful things that had ever happened to him."

This is what Max tells the judge. In order to seek to reach him, he dares to speak of the killing as "an act of *creation.*" He is not only concerned with conveying to the judge the bondage in which Bigger had lived so that it took this killing to give him "the possibility of choice, of action, the opportunity to act and to feel that his actions carried weight." He is concerned with conveying to him the sense of an impending awful catastrophe in which millions of others learn to be free through killing: "How soon will someone speak the word that resentful millions will understand: the word to be, to act, to live?"

The sense of freedom that Bigger received was only transitory. Caught and imprisoned, Bigger wonders concerning the meaning of his life. Were the intimations of freedom, of "a possible order and meaning in his relations with the people about him" real? Or would freedom and meaning elude him and would he "have to go to his end just as he was, dumb, driven, with the shadow of emptiness in his eyes"? "Maybe they were right when they said that a black skin was bad. . . . Maybe he was just unlucky, a man born for dark doom, an obscene joke."

BIGGER ACCEPTS HIMSELF

The big question of Book III is whether Bigger will find himself. It is not answered until the very end of the novel, the farewell scene with Max. "At the end," says Howe, "Bigger remains at the mercy of his hatred and fear." It is hard to make men hear who will not listen. Seven times in the last page and a half of the novel Bigger cries out to Max, "I'm all right," the last time adding, "For real, I am." The repeated assurance "I'm all right" obviously means that Bigger is not at the mercy of fear, that he is sure that he will not, as he had dreaded, have to be dragged to the electric chair, kicking and screaming, filled with animal terror because he had not been able to find human dignity. He has found what he had sought, an understanding of himself that "could lift him up and make him live so intensely that the dread of being black and unequal would be forgotten; that even death would not matter, that it would be a victory." The meaning for his life, which Max had thought to gain him the opportunity to build during life imprisonment, he had grasped from his recent experience under the duress of death.

What was the understanding of himself that he had acquired? Bone believes that Bigger casts out fear by giving himself completely to hatred, thereby in reality suffering a defeat: "What terrifies Max is that Bigger, repossessed by hate, ends by accepting what life has made him: a killer. Bigger's real tragedy is not that he dies, but that he dies in hatred. A tragic figure, he struggles for love and trust against a hostile environment which defeats him in the end." Since the conclusion has been so misunderstood, it will be necessary to quote at some length from it in order to examine it closely.

Max does not wish to talk to Bigger about the significance of his life, but he is forced to do so by Bigger's insistence. He tells Bigger: "It's too late now for you to . . . work with . . . others who are t-trying to . . . believe [in life, which is thwarted by capitalism] and make the world live again. . . . But it's not too late to believe what you felt, to understand what you felt. . . . The job in getting people to fight and have faith is in making them believe in what life has made them feel, making them feel that their feelings are as good as those of others. . . . That's why . . . y-you've got to b-believe in yourself, Bigger."

These words work upon Bigger. They give him what he wants. Ironically, however, they cause him to go further than Max intended. "Bigger, you killed," says Max. "That was wrong. That was not the way to do it." Bigger, however, accepts himself completely, including his overwhelming impulse to kill: "Sounds funny, Mr. Max, but when I think about what you say I kind of feel what I wanted. It makes me feel I was kind of right. . . . They wouldn't let me live and I killed. Maybe it ain't fair to kill, and I reckon I really didn't want to kill. But when I think of why all the killing was, I began to feel what I wanted, what I am. . . . I didn't want to kill! . . . But what I killed for, I *am*! It must've been pretty deep in me to make me kill! . . . What I killed for must've been good! . . . When a man kills, it's for something."

Max's shock on hearing these words seems excessive for one who had shown such an understanding of Bigger and had said, "We are dealing here with an impulse stemming from deep down." Perhaps this is a flaw in the scene. However, we must remember that this is the third great blow he has received. The first was when the judge, the representative of the establishment, had disregarded his desperate plea. The second was when the governor had refused to exercise clemency. These blows make it all the more difficult for him to sustain the blow inflicted by Bigger, the representative of black millions. The catastrophe he foresees seems to him more than ever inescapable.

LIBERATION COMES FROM WITHIN

Is Bigger's acceptance of his feelings of hate a victory or a defeat? If Bone is, like Max, shocked by Bigger's words, and in his shock can only see that Bigger is defeated by his hostile environment, he should consider how Bigger's killing was presented as a means of liberation and so described by Max himself. Wright, of course, is not advocating murder. Murder gave Bigger a sense of freedom, but it also gave him a sense of guilt, and, not giving him a sense of relatedness to others, it finally left him empty. But hatred of the oppressor is a natural, human emotion; it is only unhealthy when it is kept stifled. Used as the motor power of an idea driving toward a goal, it can transform both the individual and society.

So Max in his courtroom speech said of the American Revolutionary War: "Your Honor, remember that men can starve from a lack of self-realization as much as they can from a lack of bread! And they can *murder* for it, too! Did we not build a nation, did we not wage war and conquer in the name of a dream to realize our personalities and to make those realized personalities secure!". . .

Bone, moreover, overlooks completely—as does Howe—Bigger's last words before his final "good-bye": "Tell. . . . Tell Mister. . . . Tell Jan hello. . . ." Bigger does not go to death hating all white men. He accepts the comradeship of Jan, for the first time in his life dropping the "mister" in front of a white man's name. But this comradeship he will extend only to those who have earned it in action, not to superficial sympathizers, patronizing philanthropists, or bureaucratically arrogant radical sectarians. His pride in himself would not permit it otherwise.

Bigger realized in his death cell that "if there were any sure and firm knowledge for him, it would have to come from himself." And so it was. And just so, Wright indicates, the inner liberation of the blacks will have to come from within themselves. "There were rare moments," we were told early in the novel, "when a feeling and longing for solidarity with other black people would take hold of [Bigger]. . . . He felt that some day there would be a black man who would whip the black people into a tight band and together they would act and end fear and shame." Bigger in prison and in the face of death acquires the belief in himself and in his people that could propel the ghetto millions toward a goal that would catch "the mind and body in certainty and faith." Only between such blacks and such whites as Jan, the conclusion of *Native Son* implies, can there be genuine unity in a common struggle for a different and better form of society. This struggle for the third American revolution promises, in view of the adamant position of the ruling class that had rejected Max's plea and caused him to despair, to become, like the Revolutionary War and the Civil War, a bloody conflict before it is victorious.

CHAPTER 2

Characters in *Native Son*

Wright's Male Heroes and Female Characters Are Archetypes

Maria K. Mootry

Assistant professor of black American studies at Southern Illinois University at Carbondale, Maria K. Mootry defines Wright's male heroes and female characters as archetypes. In *Native Son*, Bigger is the archetype of the hero in conflict with both his environment and the archetypal women characters of the novel. Bigger's mother, like many of the mothers in Wright's fiction, represents maternal love, spiritual guidance, and support, but she is also critical and demanding. Mary Dalton represents forbidden fruit, and Bessie stands for the suffering working girl caught up in Bigger's acts of destruction. The struggles Bigger faces with these women, Mootry says, symbolize the larger conflicts of the American black experience.

Wright's fictions illustrate the maxim that the great writer has only one story to tell and he tells it over and over again. Wright's heroes, beginning with Jake Jackson, are all of a piece. Narcissistic, they value the company of men above all; they are childless; and they define themselves in opposition to women, either by using them, by perceiving themselves as being used by them, or in extreme situations, by transmuting the impulse to love to the impulse to violence and even death. . . . As James Baldwin noted in his essay, "Alas, Poor Richard," there is a space in Wright's fiction where love should be, and that space is filled with violence. If there is a difference between Wright's heroes and the other American heroes, it is that Wright's men ostensibly turn to violence out of a sense of having been violated by the racial-economic injustices of America. And the black woman, as we shall see, is perceived as a co-conspirator of the oppressor. . . .

Excerpted from "Bitches, Whores, and Woman Haters: Archetypes and Typologies in the Art of Richard Wright," by Maria K. Mootry, in *Richard Wright: A Collection of Critical Essays,* edited by Richard Macksey (Englewood Cliffs, NJ: Prentice Hall, 1984). Reprinted with permission from the author.

There is some evidence that Wright himself indulged in ... primary narcissism, although his self-centeredness reached a more subtle level. In a letter included in a tribute to Wright, Harry Birdoff recalls that Wright was "a Natty dresser." More significant is the way Wright consistently depicts himself as a superior being in the company of barely comprehending women in various autobiographical pieces. In *Black Boy*, for example, Wright recalls his encounter with two women in Memphis, Tennessee where he stops on his way north. In this episode, Wright finds himself "threatened" by the peasant mentality of his landlady, Mrs. Moss, and her daughter, Bess. Simple Bess is ready to be had and pounces on poor Richard for a prospective husband. "You like Bess, Richard?" Mrs. Moss asks at their first meeting. Richard is astounded. "What kind of people were these?" he asks incredulously. Wright dismisses poor Bess with this passage:

> Later, after I had grown to understand the peasant mentality of Bess and her mother, I learned the full degree to which my life at home had cut me off, not only from white people but from Negroes as well. To Bess and her mother, money was important, but they did not strive for it too hard. *They had no tensions, unappeasable longings, no desire to do something to redeem themselves.* The main value in their lives was simple, clean, good living and when they thought they had found those same qualities in one of their race, they instinctively embraced him, liked him, and asked no questions. But such simple unaffected trust flabbergasted me. It was impossible. [Emphasis mine.]

Bess and her mother are avatars of the feudal, simplistic Southern peasant, while Wright is the hero, on his quest to the urban industrial North. They are part of the obstacles every hero must overcome in his quest for himself. Tensionless Bess can only offer Richard food ("You can eat with us any time you like"). Food, Sex and Religion are the anodynes with which these women are associated—everything to narcotize an intelligent, questioning spirit. "Would they be angry with me when they learned that my life was a million miles from theirs?" Wright immodestly wonders.

Interestingly, it was not only the black woman who precipitated this sense of superior separateness in Wright. In his essay, "The Man Who Went to Chicago," Wright contemplates his fellow white women workers in a similar fashion. Once again we find the persona looking down at a preconsciousness that astounds him. This time he attributes the atrophied sensibilities of the female to the seduction of American materialism:

> During my lunch hour, which I spent on a bench in a nearby park, the waitresses would come and sit beside me, talking at random, laughing, joking, smoking cigarettes. I learned about their tawdry dreams, their simple hopes, their home lives, their fear of feeling anything deeply, their sex problems, their husbands. They were an eager, restless, talkative, ignorant bunch, but casually kind, and impersonal for all that. *They knew nothing of hate and fear, and strove instinctively to avoid all passion.* [Emphasis mine]

With somewhat contradictory logic, Wright finds these women workers lacking precisely because they are not "Negro":

> I often wondered what they were trying to get out of life, but I never stumbled upon a clue, and I doubt if they themselves had any notion. They lived on the surface of their days; their smiles were surface smiles, and their tears were surface tears. Negroes lived a truer and deeper life than they, but I wished that Negroes, too, could live as thoughtlessly, serenely, as they. The girls never talked of their feelings; *none of them possessed the insight or the emotional equipment to understand themselves or others.* How far apart in culture we stood! *All my life I had done nothing but feel and cultivate my feelings; all their lives they had done nothing but strive for petty goals,* the trivial material prizes of American life. We shared a common tongue, but my language was a different language from theirs. [Emphasis mine]

THE MALE HEROES

Later, Bigger Thomas would find himself besieged by a rich white girl whose vacuous life impels her to seek real experience by demanding that he act as her guide to that mysterious world of the Chicago black ghetto.

Jake and Al and Bob and Slim in *Lawd Today;* Bigger and Gus and Jack in *Native Son;* Fishbelly and his friends in *The Long Dream*—these are the communities of equals Wright constructs in his fiction. Eventually the hero, an isolato and loner, moves beyond even this community, but it is here that he is nourished and formed. Some of the conversations between males in Wright's fiction read like stream-of-consciousness passages. Man-to-man they understand the sexual jokes, the shared information, the cathartic complaints, the swagger of profanity. Language among males is an inclusive ritual for Wright; a language reserved for men only. . . .

Wright's heroes often find themselves in a state of what [Martin] Heidegger has called "throwness-into-being": they are extra-conscious, full of contingency and potentiality. If the men embody this concept, however, the women are the exact opposite; they exist in a state of prehistory, embedded inchoately in the *condition humaine*. Only to the extent that men define themselves in opposition to women are they validated as re-created, autonomous beings. If one accepts the philosophy of archetypal study, then Erich Neumann's description of the elementary character of the Negative Feminine aptly describes the pattern of male-female relationships in Wright's fiction. Neumann states:

> The phases in the development of consciousness appear then as embryonic containment in the mother, as childlike dependence on the mother, as the relation of the beloved son to the Great Mother, and finally as the heroic struggle of the male hero against the Great Mother. In other words, the dialectical relation of consciousness to the unconscious takes the symbolic mythological form of a struggle between the Maternal-Feminine and the male child, and here the growing strength of the male corresponds to the increasing power of consciousness in human development.

In one sense, Wright creates archetypes in his fiction; his characters are typologies which personify the hero in opposition to his environment, which includes "the feminine." In this sense they project a truth of the black experience, indeed of human experience.... For Wright's men and women and their conflicts are *real* in the sense that [literary critic Georg] Lukács defines realism. According to Lukács in *Realism in Our Time: Literature and the Class Struggle*:

> The literature of realism, aiming at a truthful reflection of reality, must demonstrate both the concrete and abstract potentialities of human beings.

Typology, for Lukács, is the gift of the great realist writer, more desirable than day-to-day detail. As he explains:

> Typology and perspective are thus related in a special way. The great realist writer is alone able to grasp and portray trends and phenomena truthfully in their historical development—"trends" in that area where human behaviour is moulded and evaluated, where existing types are developed further and new types emerge.

THE MALE/FEMALE CONFLICT

For a man of Wright's time, the basis of his typology, of his "unconscious possession of a perspective independent of, and reaching beyond, his understanding of the contemporary scene," lay in his perception of the de-feudalization of the black experience. Beginning with the turn of the century blacks were steadily, in spurts and waves, leaving the agrarian South with its culture in all its parameters: the folk imagination and the religious worldview. And every plot Wright devised was a commentary on this historical development; every character he created a player upon that stage. The conflicts between men and women in his fiction, while meeting Neumann's criteria for archetypal struggle, dramatizes a central conflict in the specific black experience. All of Wright's women, as has been observed of [James] Baldwin's fiction, are Mothers or Whores. As mothers, the women are equated with the Christian-Feudal-Folk element of the black experience; as whores they are associated with the abstract, formless, and isolated freedom found in a world grown increasingly technological and industrial.

Nowhere is the schematic positioning of men and women clearer than in *Native Son*. In this shocking tale of a black youth who re-creates himself through crime, Wright's naturalism congeals into archetypal typology. Bigger's well-meaning mother, like almost all of Wright's fictional mothers, represents the timidity and refuge of a folk-feudal mentality; Bigger's girlfriend, Bessie Mears, represents the deracinated worker living in the alien industrial world; and Mary Dalton, the wealthy white radical who befriends Bigger, is a nouvelle Desdemona, the bitch goddess of American success, the forbidden fruit of Marxism and white womanhood. Each is a form of consciousness, a kind of threat or conscience at the same time that they are examples of reductive feminineness; and both are threats that Bigger, in his desperate quest for manhood, must "blot out." The schema is multifaceted. Bigger is a black everyman, the hero whose essence is existential, contingent, protean; Mrs. Thomas, his mother, represents the sacred ethos epitomized in the spirituals; Bessie represents the secular culture, particularly the aesthetic and existential stance of the blues; and Mary Dalton represents the integrationist, global ethic of scientific socialism. The three women further represent three types of love: maternal, sexual or erotic, and political (platonic). In a sense, the very plot of the novel involves the encounter with and the ensuing demise of the various forms of love (including the *agape* or fraternal love of Bigger's friends), as Bigger moves toward his final "shock of recognition."

MRS. THOMAS: THE MOTHER FIGURE

Bigger's conflict with his mother and his final rejection of her maternal love belongs to a "phenomenon truthful in the historical development" of Black Americans. . . . Too often, and this is not without its positive side, but too often in the black community, Mama is an awesome blend of maternal love, spiritual authority and physical support. "We wouldn't have to live in this garbage dump if you had any manhood in you," she reminds him, at once demanding, critical, bitchy. Her faith is lost on alienated Bigger and completely ironical given the fate that awaits her son. When she sings:

> Life is like a mountain railroad
> With an engineer that's brave
> We must make the run successful
> From the cradle to the grave . . .

she does not realize how ironic her lyrics are; Bigger will go to an early grave, but no Christian *caritas* or loving engineer will give him a "successful" run. At other times, Mrs. Thomas functions as a kind of jeremiah chorus when she warns:

> ". . . mark my word, some of these days you going to set down and *cry*. Some of these days you going to wish you had made something out of yourself, instead of just a tramp. But it'll be too late then."

Bigger replies impatiently, "Stop prophesying about me.". . . Certainly Mrs. Thomas' attitude recalls the portrayal of Wright's mother in his autobiographical essay, "The Ethics of Living Jim Crow." There Wright describes how his mother beat him mercilessly when she discovered he had fought white boys. "How come yuh didn't hide?" she asked, "How come yuh always fightin'?". . . Even as Mrs. Thomas demands that Bigger act like a man she displays little confidence in him and even wonders aloud why she "birthed" him. . . .

Little wonder Bigger "escapes" this suffocating maternal "love" for the rough camaraderie of his pals. They can share fantasies while watching typical movies like *The Gay Woman* (Wright himself was fond of the cinema). All too soon, of course, Bigger's intense fears and ambivalence about indulging in street crime will disrupt even this peer-group solidarity.

MARY DALTON: THE FORBIDDEN FRUIT

Mary Dalton, Bigger's American Aphrodite, his nouvelle Desdemona, represents the dual lures of two forbidden fruits:

white womanhood and Marxist politics. At first, the "love" she offers him is almost platonic: she is the first white person to respond to Bigger as an equal; and her queries about Bigger's membership in a union imply her acceptance of Bigger as a working man. Her very simplicity "confounds" Bigger. He is not used to such uncritical attitudes, from whites or blacks. Yet there are early overtones that the Bigger-Mary attraction is "perverted": her excessive drinking and her curiosity about "black life" suggests that she associates Bigger with the sensual, the taboo. Bigger, already goaded by the blonde heroine in his afternoon film, refuses to see Mary as a person: she is the rich white girl, the real counterpart of the Ginger Rogers, Jean Harlow, and Janet Gaynor posters that decorate his room in the Dalton home. She is the American bitch goddess of success, a "whore," yet everything he has been brainwashed to believe the ultimate of femininity to be: she is beautiful, slender, and soft, much softer than Bessie. And so, in the dark and feeling warmed by too much rum, he rapes her (psychologically if not physically; there is some evidence that the rape actually occurs in an earlier version of the novel). He steals the white man's pride, he desecrates the shrine, the pristine vessel of white womanhood, he asserts his black manhood through the one force allowed him in a nay-saying society; his sexual organ.

Of course, not quite. In the South, the archetypal pattern of black-white love had led to death or literal dissolution. Wright, in a "nightmare of remembrance," recalled an episode on the job:

> One of the bell-boys was caught in bed with a white prostitute. He was castrated and run out of town. Immediately after this all the bell-boys and hall-boys were called together and warned. We were given to understand that the boy who had been castrated was a "mighty, mighty lucky bastard." We were impressed with the fact that next time the management of the hotel would not be responsible for the lives of "trouble-makin' niggers."

And so we find Bigger acting out his self-imposed role in a ritualistic American drama. When a long slow sigh goes up from the bed into the air of the darkened room, it is the final, irrevocable sigh of death, of death in love, of the death of love between black and white. In a sense, Mary Dalton becomes a kind of sacrifice: she offers herself in "love," making her death a necessity; she causes the birth of a new Bigger. In a reversal of the classical lynching pattern, she becomes the whore-as-*pharmakos*, taking on herself the sins of her society, dying that black manhood may be born.

The theme of love-and-death is equally germane to the Bigger/Bessie relationship. This relationship shows a new trend in the black experience. Lukács called for "'trends' not so much in the social and political field, as in that area where human behaviour is moulded and evaluated, where existing types are developed further and new types emerge." Bessie Mears, a maid in a white neighborhood whose only recreation is alcohol and sex, is a new type. She is the secularized blues individual; her love for Bigger is a bluesy kind of love; undemanding, with no expectations, laced with pain and an acute sense of *temporariness*. . . .

BESSIE: THE WORKING GIRL

Bessie represents "the suffering woman caught up in the web of uncontrollable destructive forces." Love, for her, becomes another form of self-immolation; already oppressed, she seeks in Bigger another oppressor—anything to assuage her sense of *anomie*. The moments when she rises above her femaleness, her vulnerability, and begins to act as a reality principle for him, are rejected by Bigger; he prefers to relate to her as an embodiment of need, of suffering, of willlessness, of mindless whoredom. He wants only erotic love from Bessie. As they walk in the snow Bigger longs to "suddenly be back in bed with her, feeling her body warm and pliant to his." But the look on her face threatens him: it is hard and distant; it asks questions. "He wished he could clench his fist and swing his arm and blot out, kill, sweep away the Bessie on Bessie's face and leave the other helpless and yielding before him."

Like Mary Dalton, in death Bessie is more meaningful to Bigger than in life. Bigger's triumph over his oppression and his transformation to a conscious hero is catalyzed by contemplating what Bessie's life *meant*. During the trial which will end in Bigger's own death sentence, he sees the totality of Bessie's life from a heightened perspective, from the perspective Lukács required of the realist writer himself "independent of, and reaching beyond, his understanding of the contemporary scene":

> . . . he felt a deeper sympathy for Bessie than at any time
> when she was alive. . . . Anger quickened in him; an old feel-
> ing that Bessie had often described to him when she had

come from long hours of hot toil in the white folks' kitchens,
a feeling of being forever commanded by others so much that
thinking and feeling for one's self was impossible.

In *Love and Death in the American Novel*, Leslie Fiedler
theorizes that "our great novelists though experts on indig-
nity and assault, on loneliness and terror, tend to avoid treat-
ing the passionate encounter of a man and woman, which we
expect at the center of a novel. Indeed, they rather shy away
from permitting in their fictions the presence of any full-
fledged mature women giving us instead monsters of virtue
or bitchery, symbols of the rejection or fear of sexuality." At
first glance, Wright does not seem to belong to this "tradition." Yet, in a curious way, his fictions do lack *passion*. Bigger Thomas is no innocent Huck, but the encounters of this
hero with females are essentially passionless. Love, in much
of Wright's fiction, and certainly in *Native Son*, is primarily
love of self—it is narcissism as a survival tactic seeking the
shock of experience. It is indissolubly linked with death, the
deaths of old selves, making way for re-created selves. However brutal and unfair to women (and to our idea of love)
Wright seems to be, we must accept his treatment of the relations between men and women for what it is: a metaphor
for the struggle of an oppressed people to deal with history
with dignity and meaning, a vision that for all of its rigid
compartmentalization into bitches, whores, and woman-
haters offers a painful and powerful truth of our history
which should never be "blotted out."

Wright's Minor Women Characters Are More Sympathetic than the Men

Kathleen Ochshorn

Literature scholar Kathleen Ochshorn of the University of South Florida disagrees with the criticism that
Wright's female characters are negative, sexist
stereotypes. In *Native Son* in particular, she claims,
black women such as Bigger's mother represent the
structure and potential comfort of the black community. Bessie, Ochshorn says, is also more than a
mindless whore; rather, she is a complex character
whose death affects readers' emotions. Finally, the
white women of *Native Son* are also sympathetic
characters; both Mary and Mrs. Dalton feel for
Bigger and want to improve his situation in life.

Richard Wright has been much criticized . . . for creating
negative female stereotypes, both white and black, in his
work generally but particularly in his novel *Native Son*. A
larger and related criticism which surfaced earlier is that in
Native Son he portrays little sense of a strong black community, of the redeeming qualities of black life. Both criticisms
address the role of the minor characters in the novel and
their relationships to Bigger. Alice Walker has said, "What
the Black Southern writer inherits as a natural right is a
sense of community." But in *Native Son,* Wright focuses on a
lone, anti-social hero who behaves brutally toward women,
both white and black.

Native Son can only be judged as a work of fiction. Clearly
it was not intended to be an idealized picture of black life in
America. Wright does not intend the female characters to be
seen as exemplars; he does not focus primarily on the fe-

Excerpted from "The Community of *Native Son*," by Kathleen Ochshorn, *Mississippi
Quarterly,* vol. 42, no. 4, Fall 1989. Reprinted with permission from Mississippi State
University.

male characters. And Bigger's treatment of women tells us about Bigger, not necessarily about Wright. Wright wants Bigger to upset the reader. He felt that earlier he had left the wrong impression in *Uncle Tom's Children*, as he explained in his now famous essay "How Bigger Was Born":

> I found that I had written a book which even bankers' daughters could read and weep over and feel good about. I swore to myself that if I ever wrote another book, no one would weep over it; that it would be so hard and deep that they would have to face it without consolation of tears.

And Wright intended Bigger to be a man without a culture. Wright claimed that "the civilization which had given birth to Bigger contained no spiritual substance, had created no culture which could hold and claim his allegiance and faith. . . ." Bigger was estranged from the black culture on the South side of Chicago and hostile to the affluent white world of the Daltons.

The charge that *Native Son* does not depict the shared experience of black life has been expressed by some of Wright's most prominent critics. James Baldwin claimed:

> Bigger has no discernible relationship to himself, to his own life, to his own people, nor to any other people—in this respect, perhaps, he is most American—

For Baldwin, Wright's relentless focus on Bigger stripped away the importance of blacks' relationships to one another. And for Baldwin none of the other characters in the book is developed sufficiently because "we are limited to Bigger's view of them, part of a deliberate plan which might not have been disastrous if we were not limited to Bigger's perceptions."

Irving Howe recognized as crucial Baldwin's criticism that Wright leaves out the shared experience of black life. For Howe, Wright's "posture of militancy, no matter how great the need for it, exacts a heavy price from the writer, as indeed from everyone else." Howe claimed a major flaw in the novel is that only Bigger is real. The others

> have little reality, the Negroes being mere stock accessories and the whites either "agit-prop" villains or heroic communists whom Wright finds it easier to admire from a distance than establish from the inside.

. . . Critics have charged that Wright's depictions of females, black or white, are sexist. For Sylvia H. Keady, Wright's women are "at the bottom of the scale of human intelligence." In general Keady says of Wright's women:

They do not exist as equal partners and full human beings but function as conveniences for the resolution or development of masculine dilemmas. This treatment of female characters is inconsistent for a writer like Wright who describes in most of his works the effects of being a member of an oppressed minority in a racist and hostile environment.

Critic Jane Davis claims that "Wright depicts women of all types, whether black or white, domineering or 'girlish,' moralistic or sexually permissive, as yielding unsatisfactory relationships and being threatening to men." Davis believes that Bigger's "mother and girlfriend, Bessie, threaten his independence."

WRIGHT'S WOMEN SUGGEST A HUMAN COMMUNITY

The charge that the female characters in *Native Son* exist primarily in relation to Bigger, the main character, is true enough. All the other characters, male and female, play minor roles. But the female characters are not as negative or stereotypical as Keady, Davis, and others have claimed. In fact, Wright uses the women characters in particular to suggest a human community of shared values and to balance the harsh focus on Bigger. In general, the women in the novel, especially the black women, are more sympathetic characters than the men.

Wright did not intend to write a novel young bankers' daughters would sentimentalize, and Bigger's life *is* depicted as brutal; the circumstances which create Bigger are quite shocking. Wright was acutely aware of the negative reaction readers would have. He knew that Bigger was

> resentful toward whites, sullen, angry, ignorant, emotionally unstable, depressed and unaccountably elated at times, and unable even, because of his own lack of inner organization which American oppression has fostered in him, to unite with the members of his own race.

Bigger was drawn from Wright's work at the South Side Boys Club in Chicago, where he observed models for Bigger Thomas. Though Bigger is isolated from his community, a community does exist among the members of the club. Despite the fact that Bigger has treated members of this community harshly and has humiliated his buddy Gus, Gus, G.H., and Jack all feel enough loyalty to and sympathy for him to visit him in jail after he kills Mary Dalton. But the black women in particular suggest a structure of black community life which ultimately touches Bigger most deeply.

Bigger's mother and Bessie are especially compelling as they struggle to deal with a hostile and hopeless environment.

MRS. THOMAS OFFERS LOVE AND COMFORT

Bigger's mother, like Wright's mother, turns to Jesus for consolation, constantly singing hymns for comfort. The hymns irk Bigger, but Wright does not demean the mother or her religion, though religion seems a cold comfort in the rat-infested home. Jane Davis claims that "the mother causes her son to be estranged from her." Bigger *is* pressured, and he hates his family "because he knew that they were suffering and he was powerless to help them." But the family's suffering, not the mother's demands, causes Bigger's alienation. The mother is more powerless than Bigger himself and has hardly caused their suffering. Throughout the novel Bigger's mother offers warmth and love, even after she knows he is a murderer. His sister, Vera, also visits him in jail, and her sobbing affects him: "Her sorrow accused him. If he could only make her go home. It was precisely to keep from feeling this hate and shame and despair that he had always acted hard and tough toward them and now he was without defense."

Bigger then acknowledges that "His family was a part of him not only in blood, but in spirit." He realizes that religion is a comfort to his mother and even wants to believe he will see her again in some afterlife. He prays with her and touches her face with his hands. His embarrassment and hatred come when he realizes that white people are staring at him as his family, friends, and the preacher lock arms around him.

BESSIE IS MORE THAN A STEREOTYPE

Bessie is the female character who has most rankled Davis and Keady, embodying for them the worst of Wright's misogyny. For Keady, Bessie is a "dull" and "mindlessly accommodating woman when she agrees to be Bigger's accomplice in his intended kidnap." For Davis, the relationship between Bigger and Bessie illustrates the "protagonist's need to have power over the woman with whom he is involved." And Davis also claims that "virtually all relationships between men and women in Wright's novels are plagued by the men's fear of women's power over them and their attempt to escape from or rebel against this power, through callousness, abandonment, or violence."

Though clearly Bigger wants to dominate Bessie, she is no mindless accomplice. She is a weak person who drinks, and she has cooperated in some of Bigger's thefts from her employer in the past. But she is quite astute in recognizing the true nature of Bigger's crime of murder and she does not readily become involved herself.

When Bigger first waves the $125 in front of Bessie she keeps asking, "Where you get all that money from?" He already fears she has "detected" something in him when she mentions Leopold and Loeb. He imagines that Bessie is "blind": "He felt the narrow orbit of her life." Soon he decides, "She might come in just handy." Bigger "felt that there were two Bessies: one a body that he had just had and wanted badly again; the other was in Bessie's face; it asked questions, it bargained and sold the other Bessie to advantage." It is the Bessie who asks questions that Bigger wants to kill. And when he raises the plot of a ransom for a supposedly kidnapped Mary, Bessie immediately fears that he has harmed the girl: "Bigger, you ain't done nothing to that girl, is you?"

Bigger sees Bessie's "round helpless black eyes" and he believes "her fear of capture and death would bind her to him with all the strength of her life." But later when he returns to Bessie's apartment she wants no more of his plan: "I ain't doing this." He blackmails her by threatening to disclose their earlier thefts: "You done helped me to steal enough from the folks you worked for to put you in jail already."

When Bigger does reveal to Bessie that he has smothered Mary, it is Bessie, not Bigger, who immediately grasps another implication of the crime: "They'll say you raped her." Later, in the most gruesome section of the novel, Bigger bashes Bessie's brains in just after forcing her to have sex. Bigger does not want to have Bessie with him on the run, and Bessie, like his mother and sister, does accuse him and makes him feel guilt. Though his violence toward Bessie is an assertion of his power as Keady suggested, Bessie is more than a convenience "for the resolution or development of masculine dilemmas." Bessie is a complex, sympathetic character whose death is deeply moving.

The minor role that Bessie's murder plays in the trial is the most poignant racism of the book. Even Bigger realizes "Her death was unimportant beside that of Mary; he knew that when they killed him it would be for Mary's death, not

Bessie's." After he is arrested, he thinks of Bessie and the milk she warmed for him, and he tries to forget her death.

THE DALTON WOMEN FEEL FOR BIGGER

The white women in *Native Son* are not without some positive characteristics. Though Bigger in jail claims he hated Mary "as soon as I saw her," earlier in the novel he had a more positive reaction. He felt "She responded to him as if he were human, as if he lived in the same world as she." In spite of her half-baked liberalism, her doll-like qualities, her attraction to the "emotion" of black people, she does react to Bigger with some warmth. She touches him on the arm, talks directly to him and when they go to Ernie's Kitchen Shack she says, "We're not trying to make you feel badly."

Mary's mother is a flat character as she wanders through the house accompanied by the ubiquitous white cat. She is a ghost-like Tiresias, inflaming Bigger's guilt. Though she had the wealth when she married Mr. Dalton, he is the one who manages the fortune and exploits the black community through the South Side Real Estate Company. When Bigger's mother begs the influential Mrs. Dalton to save her boy, Mrs. Dalton touches Mrs. Thomas's head:

> "There's nothing I can do now," Mrs. Dalton said calmly. "It's out of my hands. I did all I could, when I wanted to give your boy a chance at life, you're not to blame for this. You must be brave. Maybe it's better."

Though the speech is tinged with noblesse oblige, it is clear that Wright is trying to avoid simple stereotypes. Although her daughter has been murdered by a young black man, Mrs. Dalton feels sympathy for his mother. Even the Irish cook Peggy tries to be sympathetic to Bigger when he is first hired: "My folks in the old country feel about England like the colored folks feel about this country." The white males, except for the communists Max and Jan, are drawn quite negatively. But Wright stopped short of portraying the whole white race as hopelessly racist and cold-hearted. He created some warmth in each of the female characters.

Native Son is still a deeply disturbing book, as Wright intended it to be. Bigger is as frightening as he is inevitable and understandable. The novel also clearly identifies violence with sex, at least in Bigger's mind. Bigger's appetite for excitement and crime is described in sexual terms and his sexual feelings result in violence. Early in the novel Bigger is near "hysteria." "His entire body hungered for the keen sensation, something exciting and violent to relieve the tautness." He feels attracted to Mary right before he smothers her: he kisses her and feels her breasts. After he murders Mary and Bessie he feels that "In all of his life these two murders were the most meaningful things that had ever happened to him." Wright illustrates Bigger's intense anger and physical longing for violence as a measure of Bigger's oppression, his hopelessness in a world that has boxed him in. Bigger does lash out at women in particular; Wright does not. The author creates a number of characters, male and female, white and black, who show that a measure of humanity still exists in a racist society. While Bigger can find no real solace in his human community, Wright still creates a complex world of vivid minor characters who offer some measure of hope. The black women in particular do represent a community.

In the final scene of the novel Bigger and his lawyer share an affectionate few words and Bigger says, ". . . tell Ma I was all right and not to worry more, see? Tell her I was all right and wasn't crying none. . . ." Wright chooses to end the novel by emphasizing Bigger's deep attachment to his mother and the decent world she represents to him. Perhaps because of his own suffering, Bigger can now express a more fully developed sympathy with a female character. Particularly in the portraits of Bigger's mother and Bessie, Wright suggests that Bigger was less isolated from the community than he believed himself to be.

Bigger Thomas Is a Product of Mass Culture

Ross Pudaloff

Wayne State University assistant professor of English
Ross Pudaloff explores how the character of Bigger
Thomas is affected by mass culture. Bigger's deci-
sions about his life are informed by movies, newspapers, and detective stories rather than any intrinsic
values of his own. When he becomes a wanted and
then captured criminal, he is fascinated by press
reports of his case. He gains a sense of identity
through his brief celebrity status, adopting a tough
guy stance in the face of execution, mirroring
characters in movies and fiction of the time and
becoming, Pudaloff says, a victim of mass culture.

Bigger Thomas' story is the presentation of the fate of a
young man who takes his values from a society dominated
by movies, magazines, newspapers, and detective stories.
Every critical episode in *Native Son*, from the initial scene in
which Bigger confronts the rat to his capture and execution,
is framed, perceived, and mirrored in and through the images provided by mass culture. Bigger knows only the self
and the world mass culture presents to him. As such, Bigger
lacks the depth of character that traditionally marks the protagonist of the modern novel and whose presence in a literary character has often been used as a standard for the success or failure of a literary work. Instead, Bigger lives in a
world of images and external gestures and is himself seen in
this stereotyped way by the other characters. *Native Son* may
be said to succeed insofar as that absence of inherent character disturbs the reader by deranging his traditional con-
ception of novelistic character.

Remarkably few critics have attempted to gauge the influence of mass culture on Richard Wright. Of these, most

Excerpted from "Celebrity as Identity: Richard Wright, *Native Son*, and Mass Culture,"
by Ross Pudaloff, *Studies in American Fiction*, vol. 11, no. 1, 1983. Reprinted with permission from *Studies in American Fiction*.

observe the conventional distinction between high and mass art, seeking the moment when Wright passed from the *Argosy All-Story Magazine* and *Flynn's Detective Weekly* of his youth to the Theodore Dreiser, Gertrude Stein, and Marcel Proust of his adult life. For Michel Fabre, whose biography of Wright is the most authoritative and exhaustive available, this crucial transition occurred while Wright was living in Memphis. There "Wright did not suddenly discover his literary talents so much as he discovered good literature, represented by the great novelists of the nineteenth and twentieth centuries, in opposition to the detective stories, dime novels, and popular fiction that had been his usual fare." A glance at Wright's autobiographical writings not only confirms his stated preference for literature over popular culture but also reveals the political basis for such a preference. When he first came to Chicago in the late 1920s, Wright was astounded by more than the absence of legal segregation. In "Early Days in Chicago" he reflected upon the waitresses with whom he had worked; in his words, they would "fix their eyes upon the trash of life," an act which "made it impossible for them to learn a language that could have taught them to speak of what was in theirs or others' hearts." In the same essay, he went on to speak of "the Negro" as sharing that "lust for trash," a lust which for Wright "condemns him" to the same fate as his white counterpart.

Wright's condemnation of mass culture, however, does not mean that he felt free to disregard its effects on the individual while he went on with the business of writing literature. In his daily life he remained fascinated as well as entertained by the movies, and the interviews he gave after the publication of *Native Son* reveal his interest in photography and cinema to the extent that "he sometimes went to as many as three movies a day." That his interest in these media went well beyond recreation is apparent in the conversations he had with Harry Birdoff, whom Wright met during rehearsals for the dramatization of *Native Son* in 1941. According to Birdoff, Wright "confessed that he had not seen a single play on Broadway and said that he didn't particularly care. The movies were his 'dish.' When I questioned him, he said, 'Because I think peoples' lives are like the movies.'" Apparently Wright did not explain the meaning of this statement to Birdoff. Nevertheless, its implications can be seen in his use of mass culture as a general theme and the movies as a particular demonstration of that theme in much of his early writing. Certainly he was interested enough in the movies to bring *Native Son* to the screen as a movie, even to the point of filming it in Argentina and playing the role of Bigger himself when he was over forty years old. According to Wright, the movie "was a dream which I had long hugged to my heart and it was quite powerful until it happened."

That Wright acknowledged the impact of the literary authors of his age is not in question. What must be challenged is the assumption that the influence of popular art was negative and had to be discarded before Wright could attain any significant artistic achievement, an assumption pervasive in the criticism of his work. To call attention to the presence of references, allusions, and images of mass culture in his writings is to suggest not only a new emphasis in its content but also the presence of a different esthetic than that normally associated with this author. It is to challenge the major assumption implicit in the literary criticism of *Native Son*: "It was that rarest of coups—a work familiar in form but unfamiliar in content."

The conventional distinction between high art and popular art is missing from the writing of Richard Wright. His fiction, especially, describes worlds in which mass culture serves as the locus of personal identity. . . .

MOVIES AND NEWSPAPERS INFLUENCE BIGGER

The most obvious instance of the media's influence is Bigger's decision to accept a job with the Daltons after seeing the movie *The Gay Woman*. He gains a "great mind to take that job" and is "filled with a sense of excitement about his new job," even though he was unsure about accepting it until that moment despite the threat to cut off his family's relief if he refused. The irony is, as readers of *Native Son* have long recognized, that Bigger's movie-inspired fantasies about the Daltons correspond very well to the situation he encounters:

> Yes, his going to work for the Daltons was something big. Maybe Mr. Dalton was a millionaire. Maybe he had a daughter who was a hot kind of girl; maybe she spent lots of money; maybe she'd like to come to the South Side and see the sights sometimes. Or maybe she had a secret sweetheart and only he would know about it because he would have to drive her around; maybe she would give him money not to tell.

What Bigger cannot realize is that he is going to be taken into the lives of the Daltons. Although the specifics of their life will match those in the fantasy engendered by the movie, the Daltons and not Bigger will direct the turns of the plot. This awareness comes to him, if only dimly, when he carries a drunken Mary upstairs; he feels "as if he were acting upon a stage in front of a crowd of people."

An even more significant aspect of mass culture's influence upon Bigger occurs after Mary's death, at a time when he appears so fearful that he cannot shake down the ashes of the furnace where he disposed of her body. Bigger repeatedly desires to read the newspaper stories about the presumed disappearance of his victim. He has previously taken no interest in newspapers, with the possible exception that he may have used them to research the details of the ransom note which "he had read . . . somewhere." With the intrusion of the reporters into the Daltons' basement, however, Bigger's interest in the publicity generated by his exploits assumes overwhelming importance in his life. When he sees the newspaper on the floor of the basement, his only wish is to read, even though Mary's body is still in the furnace. As he reads it, the reality of the story, which lists her as missing or kidnapped, is persuasive, even though he knows better: "It seemed impossible that she was there in the fire, burning" if indeed the paper states otherwise.

Bigger continues to seek his identity in the newspapers even as his destiny grows progressively bleaker throughout the rest of the book. He wants to read "the story, his story" in the papers, and with this pun Wright collapses history into the contents of the front page to suggest that Bigger can understand himself only as a product of mass culture at its most destructive. Bigger searches for that "fullness" which he finds not in reality so much as in the representations of reality he encounters "when he read the newspapers or magazines, went to the movies, or walked along the streets with crowds. . . ." Accordingly, he seeks "to lose himself in it so he could find himself," but the self he finds can only be found in those images of himself that the culture presents to him.

So important is this search for an identity that Bigger devises elaborate strategies to steal a paper in order to read about himself. Yet more revealing is his decision to risk exposure by leaving his hiding place to spend his last two cents on a newspaper. Even after his capture, Bigger desires to read what the papers are saying about him. So, after he has fainted at the coroner's inquest, he awakes in his cell physically and psychologically hungry. He appeases his appetites by first eating a meal with great relish, the first since his capture, and then asking the guard for a newspaper. It can be no accident that these two forms of consumption are linked in the text. What gives Bigger the ability to live and assert himself in the world is the act of consuming what the world gives him.

Bigger's hunger after the coroner's inquest emphasizes the importance of consumption in a novel where many of the critical episodes occur during, or because of, eating and drinking. What is more, Bigger's initial response to his arrest had been to refuse to eat; his refusal can be understood as an attempt to establish a separate identity outside the power of mass culture. The scene in his prison cell also provides a perspective on Wright's use of documentary material in his fiction, what is sometimes called his "naturalism." The source for this scene is almost certainly the *Chicago Tribune*'s stories about Robert Nixon, whose murder case Wright followed from its beginning to Nixon's execution. According to the *Tribune*, Nixon showed animation only "when he spoke of food" and "when he told of having been in the movies." When Wright seized upon these seemingly dehumanizing and gratuitous details to compose his protagonist, he was not simply correcting the *Tribune*'s racism. He used them to explore the unsettling relationship between consumption and identity which they suggested to him. In 1948, Wright openly discussed the profoundly disturbing implications of consumption in mass society. Believing that it obliterated the basis for conventional political distinctions, he wrote, "The Right and Left, in different ways, have decided that man is a kind of animal whose needs can be met by making more and more articles for him to consume."

BIGGER'S CELEBRITY CREATES HIS IDENTITY

Even though Bigger ultimately rejects the newspapers on grounds that they print "the same thing over and over again," his rejection of the overt aspects of mass culture does not mean he can reject that self that has derived from the media. Much of Bigger's character is best understood as having its origin in that popular figure of thirties melodrama, the tough guy. After Mary's body is discovered in the furnace, for example, Bigger reaches for his gun, thinking to himself "he would shoot before he would let them take him;

it meant death either way, and he would die shooting every
slug he had." Since this fantasy does not materialize, it
prompts the reader to ask where the gratuitous lines come
from and what function they serve in the novel. They obviously come from gangster movies and detective stories to
shape Bigger's character; he has become what he has consumed. His attitudes about Bessie similarly mimic those of
the hard-boiled school when he thinks to himself, "a woman
was a dangerous burden when a man was running away."
Furthermore, Wright locates the source of this notion of sex
in what Bigger "had read of how men had been caught because of women." Most disastrously for Bessie, his decision
to kill her comes as much from such American myths of sex,
crime, and punishment as it does from any real danger she
poses to him. Bigger knows that "some cold logic not his
own, over which he had no control" demands her death.
This explanation of his decision speaks to an otherwise controversial aspect of the text, for Bigger is under no other immediate necessity to kill Bessie, whom, paradoxically, he
has forced to accompany him.

Wright was aware that this "logic" might elude readers
even as he was writing the novel. At the time, he lived with
Herbert and Jane Newton and read portions of the book to
Jane as he completed them. Jane objected strenuously to
Bessie's murder as "both unnecessary for the development
of the plot and insufficiently motivated." Michel Fabre offers
an explanation of Bigger's motive as proto-existentialist. The
murder, claims Fabre, exemplifies the "right to 'create,' . . .
by rejecting the accidental nature of the first murder with
further proof of his power to destroy.". . .

By 1935, when he finished "Big Boy Leaves Home,"
Wright had already critiqued the desire for an identity acquired from mass culture by contrasting it with an identity
chosen by the individual. While Big Boy is hiding in the kiln
to escape the lynch mob, he fantasizes a heroic death in
which he kills many of his attackers before the mob kills
him. The desire for revenge is unremarkable in itself. Indeed, if that were all to Big Boy's fantasy, the reader might
be tempted to place Big Boy in a more militant Afro-
American tradition than the one represented by his terror-
ized parents. Big Boy makes this impossible when he
chooses the mass media as the form for this identity: "N the
newspapersd say: NIGGER KILLS DOZEN OF MOB BE-

FORE LYNCHED! Er mabbe theyd say: TRAPPED NIGGER
SLAYS TWENTY BEFO KILLED! He smiled a little. Tha
wouldnt be so bad would it?" For a moment, Big Boy believes
as Bigger often does that celebrity creates identity. In the
story, however, the destructive effects of the fantasy are
counteracted by a community that helps Big Boy to escape.
Lacking such a community, Bigger is fatally attracted to the
identity one achieves through publicity.

Bigger's last appearance in the novel may have more in
common with the roles provided by the popular media than
with the claim he makes that "what I killed for, I *am*." The
sincerity of this sentiment, notwithstanding, it fails to distin-
guish an authentic personal identity from an identity formed
by mass culture. The very last words of the novel, a portrait
of Bigger awaiting execution after Max's departure, show
Bigger adopting the tough guy as his final identity: "He still
held on to the bars. Then he smiled a faint, wry, bitter smile.
He heard the ring of steel against steel as a far door clanged
shut.". . . The separation of the reader from the hero, the emphasis on maintaining external appearances, and the gestures of irony and alienation are all too familiar from the
tough guy of movies and fiction. If the reader leaves Bigger's
consciousness to stand totally outside him, this is so, at least
in part, because Bigger has nothing but an outside to know.

MASS CULTURE INFLUENCES OTHER CHARACTERS

Although Bigger is the most complete victim of mass culture
in *Native Son*, Wright will not allow the reader to forget that
he is emblematic rather than unique. The Daltons pay
homage to the influence of mass culture despite their wealth
and color. When they pose for newspaper photos, their behavior goes beyond any desire to communicate with their
daughter's kidnapper and procure her safe return. When the
reporters all but break into their house, they send coffee to
them, at the very least showing their enormous respect for
the power of the press, if not granting that institution the
right to invade one's house and private life.

Max, Bigger's lawyer, is the most important of these other
characters who present the world in the language of mass
culture, mainly because his role in the text has remained so
controversial. His speech to the judge provides the subject of
an ongoing critical debate over the extent to which this character speaks for Wright's position as a communist. The issue

is whether Max's speech fulfills or undercuts the ideology of the text as a whole. By examining Max's language with an eye toward its dependence on mass culture, this central issue can be redefined. His speech necessarily places Max in a world in which the effects of mass culture dominate the lives of every character. Without any specific request from Bigger, Max sends him a newspaper, an acknowledgment of Bigger's curiosity and, as it turns out, an act revealing Max's participation in his society. In the speech to the judge, he decries the invidious influence of the media. He notes "how constantly and overwhelmingly the advertisements, radios, newspapers and movies play upon us!" as he seeks to explain Bigger to the judge as well as to the reader.

Ultimately, Max is not so detached from the influence of the media as his statement would seem to indicate. He conceives his task as Bigger's lawyer in terms of constructing a sort of counter-movie to the one created by the press. As he says, "how can I, I asked myself, make the picture of what has happened to this boy show plain and powerful upon a screen of sober reason, when a thousand newspaper and magazine artists have already drawn it in lurid ink upon a million sheets of public print?" Like Bigger, and like those who seek to destroy Bigger, Max sees the world as being composed as a series of images rather than as a place filled with individual and autonomous characters. Accordingly, Max defends Bigger as the "hapless actor in this fateful drama.". . .

BIGGER'S CHARACTER IS CINEMATIC

In esthetic terms, *Native Son*'s subversion of the authenticity of character may bring it closer to a cinematic manipulation of the image than to a novelistic valorization of character. Germane to this issue is George Bluestone's argument that cinema and fiction are antithetical because they depend upon quite opposite concepts of character, a difference between the internalized characters of the novel and the externalized characters of film. In "How Bigger Was Born," Wright stated that "the burden of all serious fiction consists almost wholly of character-destiny." This statement may seem to be the only noncontroversial one in the entire essay, devoted as it is to defending criminality to the law abiding, communism to the noncommunists, and literary effort to the communists. But Bigger lacks those ingrained patterns of belief and habit that denominate character in the realist tradition and in the legacy of nineteenth-century thought. As the destiny of his character is quite different, the novel in which he works out that destiny changes accordingly. Though Bluestone's distinction may hold true for the characters of the traditional novel, it clearly breaks down to the extent that Bigger is a cinematic rather than a novelistic character.

Wright himself specifically called for literature to go "beyond the realism of the novel" in order to create a novel "bigger, different, freer, more open.". . .

Perhaps ironically, given his literary intentions and political beliefs at the time of the composition of *Native Son*, Richard Wright returned the novel to its original function as the popular expression of ordinary life, an expression which both ignores and defies the dictums of higher consciousness, whether be it political or literary.

Bigger Thomas Wants to Be Heard

James A. Miller

James A. Miller is known for his extensive writings
about Richard Wright. He is an associate professor of
English and intercultural studies at Trinity College
in Hartford, Connecticut. Miller challenges the view
that Bigger Thomas is inarticulate and requires Max
as his voice in *Native Son*. Though Bigger uses the
speech patterns of the black community, he wants
to be heard within the white community against
which he struggles to discover his own voice, which
he ultimately discovers through the use of violence.
Though Max represents Bigger during his trial, he
does not speak for Bigger directly in that he does
not actually represent his views.

Critical commentary about *Native Son* has invariably focused on the meaning of the final section of the novel, particularly Max's impassioned speech to the judge in his vain
attempt to save Bigger Thomas's life and the final encounter
between Max and Bigger at the end of the novel. Max's appearance in the novel has been regarded by many critics—
among them Irving Howe, Robert Bone, Dan McCall, Edward Margolies, and Russell Brignano—as an ideological
intrusion which disrupts the artistic unity of *Native Son*. To
the extent to which Max speaks for Bigger Thomas and, by
implication, for Richard Wright—so the argument goes—
Wright succumbs to his own ideological (i.e., political) impulses at the expense of his literary artistry. One important
consequence of the centrality some readers and critics con-
fer upon Max's role in *Native Son* is that it inevitably leads
to the conclusion that Bigger Thomas himself is inarticulate,
incapable of negotiating the conflict between "thought" and
"feeling" which defines his emotional life for a great deal of

Excerpted from "Bigger Thomas's Quest for Voice and Audience in Richard Wright's
Native Son," by James A. Miller, *Callaloo*, vol. 9, no. 3, 1986. Copyright ©1986 by
Charles H. Rowell. Reprinted with permission from Johns Hopkins University Press.

the novel, incapable of telling his own story and, therefore, of defining himself. To be sure, Bigger's story is presented from the perspective of a third-person narrator who is clearly more politically informed and verbally articulate than Bigger himself, and, within the novel itself, readers are confronted with a variety of voices—ranging from Buckley, the State's Attorney, to Max—which seek to define Bigger's reality. Nevertheless, the concluding scene of the novel clearly belongs to Bigger and his recovery of his voice at this crucial moment in *Native Son* not only undermines the argument that Max functions as a spokesman for Wright's political views but also challenges the view that Bigger himself is inarticulate.

The insistence by some critics that Max functions as authorial spokesman seems to derive from the rather mechanical equation of Max's political beliefs (and legal tactics) with those of the Communist Party and, therefore, with Wright's ideological viewpoint. But this perspective tends to overlook the artistic and ideological complexity of *Native Son* and, indeed—as Mikhail Bakhtin points out—the stylistic uniqueness of the novel as a genre: its incorporation of a range of *heterogeneous* stylistic unities into a structured artistic system. In Bakhtin's words:

> The novel can be defined as a diversity of social speech types (sometimes even diversity of languages) and a diversity of individual voice, artistically organized. . . . Authorial speech, the speeches of narrators, inserted genres, the speech of characters are merely those fundamental compositional unities with whose help heteroglossia can enter the novel; each of them permits a multiplicity of social voices and a wide variety of their links and interrelationships.

Bakhtin's definition of the novel as a multiplicity of voices is particularly useful in this context, it seems to me. It cautions us against isolating any single language system (in this case, Max's speech) as a direct and unmediated expression of authorial intention; it directs our attention to the possibility that there are other voices and communities in *Native Son* which deserve close attention; and it requires us to pay careful attention to the various speech communities Bigger Thomas encounters on his quest for voice and audience.

BIGGER IS NOT INARTICULATE

To begin with, it should be clear that Bigger Thomas is far from the inarticulate character many critics claim him to be.

Bigger is sullen, brooding, brusque, and sometimes violent
in his attitude towards his family and immediate community, but he is definitely *not* inarticulate. If we define the pattern of call-and-response in the Afro-American community
as a dynamic exchange between speaker and audience, one
which elicits responsive speech from the audience and encourages the audience to respond with its own variation on
the performer's song or story, there are numerous examples
of Bigger Thomas's participation in this pattern in *Native
Son.* Early in the novel, for example, after Bigger and Gus
have amused themselves by the ritual of "playing white," the
following exchange occurs:

> "You know where the white folks live?"
> "Yeah," Gus said, pointing eastward. "Over across the
> 'line'; over there on Cottage Grove Avenue."
> "Naw; they don't," Bigger said.
> "What you mean?" Gus asked, puzzled. "Then, where do
> they live?"
> Bigger doubled his fist and struck his solar plexus.
> "Right down here in my stomach," he said.
> Gus looked at Bigger searchingly, then away, as though
> ashamed.
> "Yeah; I know what you mean," he whispered.
> "Every time I think of 'em, I *feel* 'em," Bigger said.
> "Yeah; and in your chest and throat, too," Gus said.
> "It's like fire."
> "And sometimes you can't hardly breathe . . . ."
> Bigger's eyes were wide and placid, gazing into space.
> "That's when I feel like something awful's going to happen
> to me . . ." Bigger paused, narrowed his eyes. "Naw; it ain't
> like something going to happen to me. It's . . . like I was go-
> ing to do something I can't help . . . ."
> "Yeah!" Gus said with uneasy eagerness. His eyes were full
> of a look compounded of fear and admiration for Bigger.
> "Yeah; I know what you mean. It's like you going to fall and
> don't know where you going to land . . . ."

The ease with which Gus anticipates what Bigger is going
to say, the way their voices overlap and co-mingle in this
conversation tends to undermine Wright's assertion, in
"How Bigger Was Born," that Bigger ". . . through some quirk
of circumstance . . . had become estranged from the religion
and the folk culture of his race." Bigger, in fact, belongs to a
specific speech community within the larger black community, one which is governed by its own norms and values:
the world of the black, urban, male *lumpenproletariat* [the
disfranchised working class]. Not only is Bigger articulate in

this world, he exercises considerable power within it. Bigger realizes, perhaps more fully than Gus, Jack, and G.H., that fear and shame are the dominant forces in the world he inhabits; and, by successfully manipulating these emotions, externalizing them—as he does when he pulls his knife on Gus in the pool-room—he gains power over this world, or at least manages to keep it at bay.

BIGGER SEEKS AN AUDIENCE IN THE WHITE COMMUNITY

Bigger Thomas's quest for voice and audience has therefore little to do with his relationships with the black community, tension and conflict-ridden as they may be, but is inextricably connected to his perceptions of the white world. In other words, Bigger's quest for voice and audience is essentially Other-directed, defined by his need to struggle with externally determined definitions of the self. As Wright observes:

> To Bigger and his kind white people were not really people; they were a sort of great natural force, like a stormy sky looming overhead, or like a deep swirling river stretching suddenly at one's feet in the dark. As long as he and his black folks did not go beyond certain limits, there was no need to fear that white force. But whether they feared it or not, each and every day of their lives they lived with it; even when words did not sound its name, they acknowledged its reality. As long as they lived here in this prescribed corner of the city, they paid mute tribute to it.

The white world represents, in Bakhtin's terms, the world of "authoritative discourse":

> The authoritative word demands that we acknowledge it, that we make it our own; it binds us, quite independently of any power it might have to persuade us internally; we encounter it with its authority already fused to it. The authoritative word is located in a distanced zone, organically connected with a past that is felt to be hierarchically higher. . . . It is a *prior* discourse. It is therefore not a question of choosing it from among other possible discourses that are equal. It is given . . . in lofty spheres, not those of familiar contact. Its language is a special . . . language. . . . It is akin to taboo. . . . It demands our unconditional allegiance. . . . It enters our verbal consciousness as a compact and indivisible mass; one must either totally affirm it, or totally reject it. It is indissolubly fused with its authority—with political power, an institution, a person—and it stands and falls together with that authority.

It is within this world of "authoritative discourse"—symbolized by the billboard of the State's Attorney in the opening pages of the novel, the distortions of African reality at the

Regal Theatre, the liberal pieties of the Dalton family, the inflammatory rhetoric of the press, and the blatantly racist arguments of the State's Attorney—that Bigger must struggle to discover his voice and, presumably, an audience which will give assent to his testimony.

But what is the nature of the dialogue Bigger Thomas seeks, and with whom? As readers of *Native Son*, we know the sense of elation Bigger experiences in the aftermath of Mary Dalton's accidental death, the ease with which he accepts responsibility for his action and confers meaning upon it, the way in which his secret knowledge establishes further distance between himself and his family, the sense of power he temporarily achieves over a white world trapped smugly in its own assumptions of racial superiority; yet, one of the questions which has always intrigued me as a reader is: why doesn't Wright allow Bigger Thomas to escape, say somewhere between the first and second books of *Native Son?* What would be the imaginative and ideological implications of Wright exercising such an artistic choice? The text of the novel provides us with a clear answer:

> He wanted suddenly to stand up and shout, telling them that he had killed a rich white girl, a girl whose family was known to all of them. Yes; if he did that a look of startled horror would come over their faces. But, no. He would not do that, even though the satisfaction would be keen. . . . He wanted the keen thrill of startling them, but felt that the cost was too great. He wished that he had the power to say what he had done without the fear of being arrested; he wished that he could be an idea in their minds; that his black face and the image of his smothering Mary and cutting off her head and burning her could hover before their eyes as a terrible picture of reality which they could see and feel and yet not destroy. He was not satisfied with the way things stood now; he was a man who had come in sight of a goal, then had won it, and in winning it had seen just within his grasp another goal, higher, greater. He had learned to shout and had shouted and no ear had heard him.

Bigger will not be satisfied, in other words, until his actions are recognized by the world whose attention he seeks. And it is here that we see how completely Bigger's quest for voice and audience are determined by his fascination with the white world.

For Bigger, in fact, *does* achieve recognition for his actions from his girlfriend, Bessie. As we know, Bessie remains an unacknowledged character—except as evidence—by the State's

Attorney, by Max, and by many critics as well, yet she is an important figure in Bigger's life. Like Gus, Jack, and G.H. she participates in Bigger's world and understands its terms. Bessie knows Bigger so well that she realizes fairly quickly that he has murdered Mary Dalton and elicits a confession from him. Enlisted by Bigger as an unwilling accomplice in his inept kidnapping scheme, Bessie articulates the pain of her life with all of the passion of a blues singer, a testimony to which Bigger nods his head and assents, but a song which he clearly does not want to hear. And when Bigger rapes and murders Bessie, he effectively severs his ties to the black community. From this point in the novel until its conclusion, Bigger functions essentially as a soloist.

MAX DOES NOT SPEAK FOR BIGGER

It is in this context that Max emerges in *Native Son* as an intermediary between Bigger Thomas and the white world. Throughout the novel, Bigger's voice falters in the presence of white people: in his encounter with Mr. and Mrs. Dalton; with Peggy, the housekeeper; with Mary and Jan, with Britten and Buckley. Virtually all of these exchanges are conducted in the interrogatory mode, with Bigger confining himself to terse, monosyllabic responses. Max interrogates Bigger too, but the difference between Max and the other white characters Bigger encounters is that Max addresses Bigger as a human being rather than as a social type. This is clearly the kind of human encounter for which Bigger has been yearning throughout the novel, one which has been presumably missing up until this point, and Bigger instinctively and immediately places his trust in Max. Nevertheless, while Max and Bigger communicate reasonably well in their private conversations, Max's defense of Bigger in the public sphere reveals that Max, too, suffers from some of the limitations of the white world.

There is, first of all, the problem of the legal strategies Max chooses to pursue in his defense of Bigger Thomas. In his review of *Native Son* for the New York *Sunday Worker,* Benjamin Davis, a leading black official in the American Communist Party during the 1940s, correctly pointed out that Max's defense of Bigger is seriously flawed and, in fact, atypical of the kind of legal defense the Communist Party would conduct. Max does not challenge the false charge of rape against Bigger Thomas, he pleads Bigger guilty to both the rape and murder of Mary Dalton, even though it is clear that the murder is accidental. Finally—Davis concludes— "Max should have argued for Bigger's acquittal in the case, and should have helped stir the political pressure of the Negro and white masses to get that acquittal."

Secondly, there is the question of whether Max fully understands Bigger Thomas. It is true that Max's probing questions awaken Bigger to a sense of his own reality which he has not experienced before, but it is also clear—as Donald Gibson has pointed out—that Max is primarily concerned with the social and symbolic implications of Bigger's situation while Bigger is concerned with his personal fate. Max *appropriates* many of the statements Bigger makes and incorporates them into the structure of his appeal to the judge, but it is clear that Max's argument will fall on deaf ears. Not only is Bigger's ultimate fate at the hands of the court a foregone conclusion, it is also clear that Bigger himself does not grasp the meaning of Max's speech.

Indeed, throughout the third book of *Native Son*, Bigger Thomas remains curiously detached from the action; he functions as a witness, an auditor to the public debate which rages about him, but not as a participant in the dialogue. The public exchanges between Max and the State's Attorney, Buckley, represent two attempts to define, in opposing ideological terms, the meaning of Bigger Thomas's actions—and, by extension, his existence—in the public sphere of "authoritative discourse." In the final analysis, however, Bigger repudiates both arguments—as we see in the concluding conversation between Max and Bigger, when Bigger blurts out: "What I killed for, I *am!*" and Max backs away from him, groping for his hat like a blind man.

Max does not speak for Bigger Thomas, nor does he speak for Richard Wright. He attempts to *represent* Bigger, in both a legal and linguistic sense, and fails. Nevertheless, Max's presence in the novel does have an important bearing on the development of Bigger's consciousness. Through his relationship with Max, Bigger Thomas is able to further de-mystify the power of the white world over him, a process which has been unfolding since the accidental murder of Mary Dalton. And even though Bigger does not understand Max's language, he nevertheless appropriates it for his own purposes.

"The word in language," Bakhtin observes, "is half someone else's. It becomes one's own only when the speaker populates it with his own intentions, his own accent, when he appropriates the word, adapting it to his own expressive and semantic intention. Prior to this moment of appropriation, the word . . . exists in other people's mouths, in other people's contexts, serving other people's intentions: it is from there that one must take the word, and make it one's own," seizing it and transforming it into private property.

AN AUDIENCE OF NONE

This is precisely what Bigger Thomas does in the concluding pages of *Native Son*. Having shaken the "authoritative discourse" of the white world to its foundations and triggered off an ideological debate which seeks to define his place in the public sphere, Bigger Thomas, partly inspired by Max's rhetoric, chooses a position that places him decisively outside of the existing social framework.

Nevertheless, Bigger Thomas's achievement of the voice he assumes at the end of the novel has not been without its price. In cultural terms, the strategies Bigger pursues to evade white society after Mary Dalton's death—particularly the gratuitous murder of Bessie—only serve to isolate him from the black community. In social and political terms, Bigger's actions not only invite the wrath of a racist society but confirm his place within popular mythology. In personal terms, Bigger seems to achieve a level of human recognition—of sorts—through his relationships with Jan and Max, accepting Jan's offer of comradeship by, for the first time in his life, dropping the use of "mister" in front of a white man's name. But Max—as we have seen—recoils from Bigger's final speech, and the call which Bigger issues in his assertion "I Am" does not receive responsive testimony from Max. Rather, we are left with the final image of Bigger Thomas facing his impending death in proud and lonely isolation, a soloist listening to the sound of his own song.

Bigger Thomas Represents the Social Plight of the Lower Classes

James Robert Saunders

James Robert Saunders, assistant professor of English at the University of Toledo, explains the ways in which the character of Bigger Thomas represents the social plight of the lower classes in America. Bigger is stunted in society by the effects of slavery and the segregation that prevents him from accessing the same opportunities as whites. Though readers do not condone Bigger as a murderer, they understand what drives him to violence and feel that his character, forcing itself out from under the weight of oppression, has universal appeal.

In an article entitled "Richard Wright's Blues," which is included in his volume of essays, *Shadow and Act*, Ralph Ellison describes what he regards as a "basic ambiguity" in Richard Wright's sensational *Native Son*. Ellison, a contemporary of Wright's who survived to evaluate new generations of black American writers, assessed it as a crucial flaw that "Wright had to force into Bigger's consciousness concepts and ideas which his intellect could not formulate." That complaint stems from Ellison's belief that Wright compromised too much of his own personality to achieve the fundamental theme of Bigger Thomas' frustrated existence.

BIGGER IS STUNTED BY SOCIETY

To determine the validity of Ellison's complaint one must ask who is Bigger Thomas and why did the author find it necessary to create such a terrifying character? The novel might just as easily have been an American romance or at

Excerpted from "The Social Significance of Wright's Bigger Thomas," by James Robert Saunders, *College Literature*, vol. 14, no. 1, 1987. Reprinted with permission from West Chester University.

least a tale of people managing to find some solace in the midst of a world that has become increasingly complex. Wright, however, chose to give us an unpleasant view of American life, and thus the controversial anti-hero Bigger Thomas was created. The author in his introduction, "How Bigger Was Born," explains, "What made Bigger's social consciousness most complex was the fact that he was hovering unwanted between two worlds—between powerful America and his own stunted place in life—and I took upon myself the task of trying to make the reader feel this No Man's Land." Perhaps the key word in this explication is "stunted," for one must wonder about the absurdity of Thomas' position in a society that we sing about as being "the land of the free" and praise as being an endless source of opportunity. How did Bigger Thomas evolve in this much heralded land?

Of course we could look back into America's past and put the blame for the evolution of Bigger Thomas squarely on the institution of slavery. We would to some degree be correct in offering that as the reason for various ills that continue to accrue to the black race even to this day. Michel Fabre, in his definitive biography of the author, notes that Wright thought of the average black person as exceptional merely for having survived the racist circumstances of American life. More specifically, one need only delve into the background of the artist himself. Having been born on a plantation near Natchez, Mississippi, in 1908, Wright remembers, in the autobiographical *Black Boy,* that when he was a child, "Hunger had always been more or less at my elbow when I played, but now I began to wake up at night to find hunger standing at my bedside, staring at me gauntly." Decades after slavery had officially ended, blacks continued to suffer from the deprivation associated with a race struggling to advance beyond the lowest socio-economic level that any group in this country has ever experienced. As the son of a sharecropper, one step removed from slavery, young Wright directly felt the pain. . . .

As a depiction of human flaws, . . . *Native Son* is crucial to an understanding of human nature in the midst of dire circumstances. Upon committing two hideous murders, Thomas marvels:

> *He* had done this. *He* had brought all this about. In all of his life these two murders were the most meaningful things that had ever happened to him. He was living, truly and deeply,

no matter what others might think. . . . Never had he had the
chance to live out the consequences of his actions.

Frustrated by his limited position in society, the black chauffeur seems destined to kill the wealthy white Mary Dalton
and equally destined to murder the unsuspecting Bessie
Mears, whose meaning in life is similarly limited to all the
liquor and sex that Thomas can provide.

BIGGER'S CHARACTER IS UNIVERSAL

It is fairly safe to say that Dalton's death is an accident; however, as students in one of my black literature classes
agreed, that death seems too much to be pre-ordained, as if
there is no other way the restricted relationship between
Thomas and Dalton could have ended. Once he chooses to
deliver the intoxicated Dalton daughter to her bedroom, his
fate is sealed. And then it is only in the ordinary course of
events that he will take that other life, Bessie's, which had
appeared to be as lacking in meaning as his own. It is a powerful statement about the society in which we live that any-
one would have to murder to achieve some semblance of
identity. Nevertheless, we know that being a murderer has in
some sense satisfied what had been Thomas' desperate
yearning to be somebody, and we can only guess at just how
many criminals have felt the same.

In talking about Thomas in a college class composed almost equally of whites and blacks, I found it interesting that
nearly everyone sympathized with what he was going
through. Students between the ages of eighteen and sixty-five
(including an elderly Jewish woman who had to sell her
downtown business establishment because of rising crime)
declared that they understood what drove him to the depths
of depression where the novel ends. They feared him, and yet
they understood him. As strange as it might sound to some,
Bigger Thomas and his plight do have universal appeal.

Wright himself echoed the disillusionment of many when
he fled with his wife from the United States in 1946 to live in
Paris. Generally speaking, he left to avoid any further suffering of racial oppression; much like Bigger Thomas, he
was denied the opportunity to pursue individual identity, ir-
respective of race. . . .

It is not unreasonable to suspect that in a way the fictional
Native Son takes up where the autobiographical *Black Boy*
leaves off. We find the sharecropper's son fleeing his op-

pressive South to find a better life in the North. Yet Chicago proves to be no "promised land." And the story of Bigger Thomas is the tale of many an American who has ventured into unchartered territory, seeking the good life promised by our national creeds and slogans.

Some do succeed in their quests, but *Native Son* tells of how it is for countless others who fail. For those who are offended by the violence in that novel, it is essential to consider the words of John Reilly who, in his afterword to *Native Son*, declares—

> violence is a personal necessity for the oppressed. When life in society consists of humiliation, one's only rescue is through rebellion. It is not a strategy consciously devised. It is the deep, instinctive expression of a human being denied individuality.

The humiliation Reilly mentions is conveyed most effectively by Wright as he portrays the shattered life of Bigger Thomas. Yet the novel is indicative of more than just one man's predicament; it tells about the plight of blacks in general and of others who compose the lower classes. As the author gives Thomas a certain capacity for insight, we are made to question the motivation for violent action and made to perceive how alienation can result in catastrophic social harm.

CHAPTER 3

The Power of Place in *Native Son*

Native Son Is Set in a Gothic Ghetto

Robert Butler

Robert Butler's book *Richard Wright's* Native Son: *The Emergence of a New Black Hero* was published in 1992. He is professor of English at Canisius College, Buffalo, New York. Butler explores how Bigger Thomas's environment, a kind of gothic ghetto, reflects the fear and horror of his inner life. Bigger feels that he inhabits a small, restricting corner of a city otherwise bustling with opportunity for whites. His own community is a nightmare of skeleton buildings, a dark, grim reality in which he feels paralyzed and trapped.

Richard Wright, in order to suggest the extremity of his hero's radically alienated consciousness, describes the city in *Native Son* as a gothic mindscape reflecting the fear and horror that dominate his protagonist's life. Surrealistic techniques are extensively used to dramatize the fundamental lack of connection between Bigger Thomas and the world in which he is placed. Because his external life offers him so little, Bigger perceives the city as a process of fragmentation and dislocation, a strange nether world that threatens to destroy him. . . .

Because Wright was intent on filtering external experience through Bigger's radically alienated consciousness, he describes Chicago with very few coordinates in time and place. We are never given a precise idea of the year in which the novel takes place and we do not see much of the actual physical characteristics of the city in which Bigger lives. Washington Park is used for one important scene but is never clearly described. Full, coherent descriptions of streets, houses, stores, schools and other important landmarks are never given. The novel's second scene, which de-

Excerpted from "Farrell's Ethnic Neighborhood and Wright's Urban Ghetto: Two Visions of Chicago's South Side," by Robert Butler, *MELUS,* vol. 18, no.1, 1993. Reprinted with permission from *MELUS.*

scribes Bigger leaving his family's apartment and walking the street, provides a vivid example of Wright's highly selective method of depicting city life. The few details mentioned are designed more to suggest what Bigger is thinking and feeling than to establish the setting in any mimetic way. Frustrated that his environment does not present him with "a wider course of action," Bigger's attention is drawn to a streetcar rattling over "steel track." This sense of confinement is intensified when he looks up at an election poster for District Attorney, which reminds blacks that "If you break the law you can't win." When Gus and Bigger meet on a street corner, their sense of entrapment is further underscored by the "wall" they lean up against. Observing the high-flying planes and fast-moving automobiles, which painfully remind them of the mobility and possibility extended to whites in American society, they realize that black people have been placed in "one corner of the city" that amounts to little more than a "jail.". . .

Bigger is never allowed to feel a sense of continuity between himself and the world around him. . . . Bigger psychologically recoils from Chicago, which he perceives as "that vast city of white people." Just as he is about to kill Bessie, for example, he retreats into the darkness of his mind, feeling that "the city did not exist." Driving Mary and Jan through Washington Park, and becoming enveloped in his own fears and anxieties, "his sense of the city and the park fell away; he was floating in the car." As Bigger makes his escape from the Daltons' home, he sees the city vaguely as "a strange labyrinth, a chaos" which is a vivid reflector of his own tormented mind.

WRIGHT'S GOTHIC DESCRIPTIONS

To emphasize further this dislocated quality of Bigger's perceptions, Wright uses Gothic imagery extensively to describe urban reality. This is especially true in Book II where Bigger is overwhelmed by the fears that were triggered in Book I. Going to Bessie's house to draft a ransom note, he perceives the street lamps as "hazy balls of light frozen into motionlessness." After killing Mary, he passes by buildings that appear to him as "skeletons . . . white and silent in the night." In the scene immediately following his brutal murder of Bessie, Bigger wanders the streets caught in a nightmarish world where deserted buildings look like "empty skulls" and where the windows of these buildings "gaped blackly like . . . eye sockets.". . . .

Bigger Thomas's city never provides him with . . . refreshment. Instead of offering him a sense of space that enlarges his possibilities or poetic glimpses of beauty that arouse his deepest human impulses, Bigger's Chicago is a "world of steel and stone," "a strange labyrinth," which first confuses and then traps him. When he looks up at the skies . . . he sees "a cole dark-blue oval cupping the city like an iron palm." When he looks out windows, . . . he sees signs of entrapment—dark clouds that "swallow the sun," and sinister alleys leading nowhere.

Bigger's first assignment as a chauffeur is when he drives Mary and Jan through various parts of Chicago at night. . . . Observing the lake from the car window, he perceives it only as "a huge flat sheet of dully gleaming water.". . . He eventually turns off Outer Drive at Forty-seventh and Indiana Streets and drives westward through a desolate racial ghetto with "tall and dark apartment buildings looming" on either side of him. . . . He eventually passes through Washington Park, where he shares a bottle of whiskey with Jan and Mary who are making love in the back seat of the fast-moving car. The park . . . is for Bigger a grim reflection of the irrational forces lurking beneath the surface of his consciousness. As Bigger becomes intoxicated and sexually aroused, he begins to feel the life around him as a dream world that is only lightly attached to reality. His "sense of the city and park fell away," and he begins to feel that he is not driving "but simply floating away smoothly through darkness."

Leaving the park and driving north on Cottage Grove Avenue, he drops off Jan on Forty-sixth Street, a block away from the Dalton home. In a few brief minutes, the volcanic emotions and instincts that have been stirred in Washington Park will erupt with devastating results. Bigger and Mary, nearly drunk, attempt to make love in her bedroom, but this potentially romantic scene is quickly inverted into a grisly killing when Mrs. Dalton surprises the two. . . .

METAPHORIC WEATHER AND DARKNESS

There is only one point in *Native Son* where lyrical images of the city are employed—the scene early in the novel where Bigger and Gus relax on a street corner. But such imagery is used reductively to point up some bitter ironies about Bigger's situation. As he and Gus gaze upward to contemplate the clouds drifting in an open sky, they are clearly reminded that the world available to them is quite closed. Although Bigger wants to "fly," not only by becoming an aviator but also by achieving the upward mobility he has glimpses of in films, he knows that American society extends such options only to whites. Just as the space of the open sky reminds him of his own closed existence, the uncharacteristically warm afternoon serves as a reminder of the coldness of the slum housing he is forced to live in. As he remarks to Gus, "you get more heat from this sun than from them old radiators at home."

Aside from this one moment of ironic warmth and sunlight, Bigger's city provides little but extreme coldness and darkness. . . . The important scenes in *Native Son* are played out almost entirely on grimly dark nights when it is snowing. When Mary is killed late at night, Chicago receives its largest snowfall of the year. Bessie literally freezes to death after being bludgeoned by Bigger in a dark, abandoned building. Bigger, who will die at midnight, the victim of "a cold and distant world," is arrested at night after he is nearly frozen by jets of water that the police spray at him. Even when Bigger tries to escape from this dark, frozen environment, he is paralyzed. Leaping out the second floor window of the Dalton house after Mary's bones have been found in the furnace, he confronts more of the same world intent on "freezing" him:

> He turned to the window and put his hands under the upper ledge and lifted; he felt a cold rush of air laden with snow. He heard muffled shouts downstairs and the inside of his stomach glowed white hot. . . . He groped to the window and climbed into it, feeling the chilling blast of snow. He was in the air a moment; then he hit. It seemed at first that he hit softly, but the shock of it went through him, up his back to his head and he lay buried in a cold pile of snow, dazed. Snow was in his mouth, eyes, ears; snow was seeping down his back. His hands were wet and cold. Then he felt the muscles of his body contract violently, caught in a spasm of reflex action, and at the same time he felt his groin laved with warm water.

What Wright suggests by this epiphany is the absolute hopelessness of Bigger's situation. Caught in an environment that paralyzes him by depriving him of significant sight, speech, and hearing, Bigger is forced into self-destructive reflex actions, symbolized here by his urinating on himself when his warm body is shocked by the "cold" world around him. . . .

In the final analysis, Wright's city is a place defined by absences, dark nights, empty streets and abandoned buildings that become a powerful symbol of "a world whose metaphysical meanings had vanished.". . .

Wright, in order to portray the more extreme and stark world his central character is forced to confront, described Chicago's South Side in Gothic terms as a racial ghetto that became for him a terrifying revelation of a racist society intent on destroying blacks by systematically depriving them of adequate "warmth" and "light."

Man's Need for Community: The Failure of the City in *Native Son*

Charles W. Scruggs

Charles W. Scruggs teaches black American literature at the University of Arizona. Scruggs is the first
to argue that Max and Buckley of *Native Son* represent contrasting voices of the city. Symbolically, the
city represents the promised land of opportunity,
the traditional values of American society. Max
maintains that Bigger can find fulfillment in this
ideal city; for Bigger, however, the city remains a
land of segregation and fear, a place that Buckley
prophesizes will destroy him.

No one has considered Bigger's relationship to Max and to
State's Attorney Buckley as voices which represent two con-
ceptions of the city. Wright has deliberately juxtaposed three
scenes from a window, each offering a view of the streets and
buildings beyond. In the first, Bigger is alone and tries to perceive meaning in the city, but finds none. In the next, Buckley calls Bigger's attention to a city he already knows, the city
which threatens to destroy him. Finally, Max describes an
ideal city, a dream for the future in which Bigger can find fulfillment as a human being. The novel's main theme is not
man versus society, in which Bigger is an heroic or anti-
heroic rebel in the Romantic tradition. Its real theme is as old
as the Greco-Roman world: man's need for human community and, in this case, the city's failure to provide it.

THE CITY IS THE PROMISED LAND

Wright was thoroughly familiar with the actual city of
Chicago: with its stockyards and sooty factories, its gangland
killings, its storefront churches, its cynical politics. But he
also knew its mythical possibilities. Chicago was a young

Excerpted from "The Importance of the City in *Native Son*," by Charles W. Scruggs, *A
Review of International English Literature*, vol. 9, no. 3, 1978. Reprinted with permission from The University of Calgary.

city, if one measured it by years, yet it was old as all great
cities are old, "old enough," Wright said, "to have caught
within the homes of its long, straight streets the symbols and
images of man's age-old destiny, of truths as old as the
mountains and seas. . . ." Remembering his impressions of
Chicago as a young man fresh from the South, he said:

> . . . there is an open and raw beauty about that city that seems
> either to kill or endow one with the spirit of life. I felt those
> extremes of possibility, death and hope, while I lived half
> hungry and afraid in a city to which I had fled with a dumb
> yearning to write, to tell my story.

Wright fled to Chicago as others of his race had fled to the
cities of the North. Modern black literature is filled with indictments of the "promised land," and no one has written
harsher indictments than Wright himself. Yet even in his disappointment he could describe Chicago as a place to fulfill
man's potentialities. Wright's experience falls into the pattern of experience of Western man.

The history of the city in our culture has expressed both
the best and worst sides of human nature. The city organized aggression in ways which the village could not. It was
civilized man who created war, and he also created the attitudes accompanying war, one of which is that only "by
wholesale human sacrifice can the community be saved."
On the other hand, the city has often embodied man's lofti-
est dreams. It has represented his attempt to find happiness
by sharing his life with others. . . .

Near the end of the second section of *Native Son*
("Flight"), Wright used dialectical opposites to describe
Chicago. Having become a fugitive, a murderer in hiding,
Bigger reflects upon his life: "Sometimes, in his room or on
the sidewalk, the world seemed to him a strange labyrinth
even when the streets were straight and the walls were
square; a chaos which made him feel that something in him
should be able to understand it, divide it, focus it." As he lies
concealed in a room of an abandoned tenement, the early
morning light interrupts his reverie, and he jumps up to look
out the window:

> The snow had stopped falling and the city, white, still, was a
> vast stretch of rooftops and sky. He had been thinking about
> it for hours here in the dark and now there it was, all white,
> still. But what he had thought about it had made it real with
> a reality it did not have now in the daylight. When lying in the
> dark thinking of it, it seemed to have something which left it

when it was looked at. Why should not this cold white world rise up as a beautiful dream in which he could walk and be at home, in which it would be easy to tell what to do and what not to do? If only someone had gone before and lived or suffered or died—made it so that it could be understood! It was too stark, not redeemed. . . .

. . . In this scene Bigger looks at the city and sees only its cruel indifference, the inscrutable maze which expresses the bewilderment of its black inhabitants.

BIGGER'S SEGREGATED CITY

The first section of *Native Son* ("Fear") shows the city as a closed society. Not regarding Bigger and his people as human, the real city shoves them from sight. It herds them into a carefully defined space, and then ignores them. Yet, like [Goerge] Orwell's London in *1984*, it intimidates the members of this sub-human world in subtle ways. The enormous billboard of the State's Attorney points a finger at the black community and says, "IF YOU BREAK THE LAW, YOU CAN'T WIN."

Growing up in the slums of Chicago's South Side, Bigger has lived in a constant state of fear. Its ramifications spread like ripples in a pond, so that Bigger hated and feared everyone, even members of his own black family. He hid behind a mask of toughness so as not to acknowledge the full extent of this fear, for if he knew "what his life meant . . . he would either kill himself or someone else."

But Chicago not only creates fear, it also causes frustration. It holds forth its gifts and then withdraws them. "It was not," Wright says, "that Chicago segregated Negroes more than the South, but that Chicago had more to offer, that Chicago's physical aspect—noisy, crowded, filled with the sense of power and fulfillment—did so much more to dazzle the mind with a taunting sense of possible achievement that the segregation it did impose brought forth from Bigger a reaction more obstreperous than in the South." Bigger feels a momentary sense of wholeness when he shares the city through its movies or its newspapers, but the reality of his situation soon changes this feeling to discontent.

Mary Dalton's world symbolizes everything that Bigger saw in the movies, and it is just as unattainable. The fact that she has treated him as a human being, at the same time that she clung to the traditional symbols of wealth and authority, only makes Bigger feel his degradation all the more: ". . . after they had shunted him off into a corner of the city to rot and die, they could turn to him, as Mary had that night in the car, and say: 'I'd like to know how your people live.'"

When Bigger murders Mary it is an accident, but Wright makes it clear that killing is an act Bigger had often committed in his mind. After Mary's death he feels released from the terrible tightness in his chest. He feels alive, more free than ever before. He is a "man reborn." He has "created a new world for himself."

So much attention has been given this "new world" that one critic has argued that the novel is "essentially ended" after the second section. Yet as the third section opens, Bigger is numb with despair. His new self, which was based upon hatred, has not sustained him. He hungers for another set of values to give his life meaning, "a vast configuration of images and symbols whose magic and power could lift him up and make him live so intensely that the dread of being black and unequal would be forgotten; that even death would not matter, that it would be a victory."

MAX AND BUCKLEY REPRESENT TWO CITY VIEWS

Exhausted and dejected, Bigger is shown a second view of the city by State's Attorney Buckley. Counting on being re-elected if Bigger is convicted of murder in the first degree, Buckley visits him in his cell and pretends to befriend him. He "led Bigger to a window through which he looked and saw the streets below crowded with masses of people in all directions. 'See that, boy? Those people would like to lynch you. That's why I'm asking you to trust me and talk to me. The quicker we get this thing over, the better for you.'" Buckley offers Bigger safety from the mob if he confesses. The scene he points to is a city of hatred which provides Bigger with no alternative but to hate in return. Even if Buckley's false promise were true, his protection would further isolate Bigger from the human community and an understanding of himself.

Boris Max also befriends Bigger, but he does not pretend to offer him safety. Instead he gives Bigger those "images and symbols" he wants by insisting that Bigger articulate his reasons for having killed Mary. In probing Bigger's innermost feelings Max treats him as a human being, but in such a way that Bigger "felt a recognition of his life, of his feelings, of his person that he had never encountered before." Bigger now tries to "see himself in relation to other men, a thing he had always feared to try to do, so deeply stained was his mind with the hate of others for him." He wonders if there are others outside his cell who struggle as he does, and he envisions himself

> standing in the midst of a vast crowd of men, white men and black men and all men, and the sun's rays melted away the differences, the colors, the clothes, and drew what was common and good upward toward the sun. . . . Had he been blind all along? . . . Was there some battle everyone was fighting, and he had missed it?

Agonized by the thought of having never really lived, he now for the first time desperately wants to live.

After the governor has refused Max's plea for clemency, Max goes to Bigger's cell, where communication seems impossible. Anxious for more than consolation, Bigger asks Max, ". . . how can I die!" Max tries to make Bigger see that he must join the human community in spirit if he is to be saved. He takes Bigger to the window of his cell and points to the tall buildings of downtown Chicago. He tells Bigger that human hopes have built those skyscrapers and that faith in dreams keeps them from falling. A few men, he continues, have gotten control of the buildings and blocked the entrances. "But men," he said, "men like you, get angry and fight to re-enter those buildings, to live again." He asks Bigger to believe in himself, to know that his feeling of anger is warranted. Furthermore, he wants Bigger to see his life joined with others in humanity's struggle to fulfill itself. To strive and resist oppression is human, but to kill is wrong.

Max's speech is a classic statement of humanistic ideals. That Wright intended this interpretation of Max is clear from the archetypal "visionary" setting in which he places his two characters. Max has painted a picture of the earthly paradise and has shown it to Bigger in the hope that he might vicariously participate in it. . . .

BIGGER REJECTS HIS COMMUNITY

The ending of the novel is brought into perspective if we see Max's vision of the human community in conflict with Bigger's need to understand his own life. When Bigger rejects Max's vision, he does not reject Communism, he rejects the traditional values of Western civilization as symbolized by the city. Specifically, he rejects the *community* because it is less necessary to him than his own identity, his own humanity, which the real city has denied him. He tells Max that he does believe in himself, because that is the only thing he has left. He also knows *why* he killed: ". . . when I think about what you say I kind of feel what I wanted. It makes me feel I was kind of right. . . . They wouldn't let me live and I killed. Maybe it ain't fair to kill, and I reckon I really didn't want to kill. But when I think of why all the killing was, I begin to feel what I wanted, what I am." He now knows that he killed because he wanted to live not as an animal but as a human being. Conscious or unconscious, killing was an assertion of his human identity against those who had treated him as though he were merely a rat in a maze.

Bigger accepts his fate, but Max is visibly shaken. His "eyes were full of terror" and he "groped for his hat like a blind man." Ironically, Max has been the midwife at the rebirth of Bigger Thomas. His Socratic questions have made Bigger see that it is right to fight for one's humanity, even unto death. The emotion Wright depicts in Max is something akin to Aristotle's tragic "fear": "There but for the grace of God go I." In leading Bigger to a discovery of himself, Max has caught a brief glimpse of Bigger's world, and the irrationality of that world has frightened him. Max is basically a rational man, who believes in man's capacity to recognize evil and to remove it. Bigger recognizes evil as an inextricable part of his life. Not only does Max recoil from such a nightmare vision of reality, but he also knows that he is, in part, responsible for its existence.

The final parting of Max and Bigger reveals the tragic situation to both men. Max has held out two possibilities for Bigger: self-knowledge, and a share in the human community. Bigger has achieved the first, but it is a Pyrrhic victory. He is at peace with himself and has no hatred in his heart, but his "bitter smile" as he watches Max go indicates that he knows murder has placed him beyond the pale of human fellowship.

ALL THE DEMONS OF THE CITY

That the city remains blind to its sins is as much a part of the novel's impact as Bigger's acceptance of himself as a killer. Wright admitted that he had placed Max in Bigger's cell to register the moral "horror of Negro life in the United States," and he went on to explain that "we have in the oppression of the Negro a shadow athwart our national life dense and heavy enough to satisfy even the gloomy broodings of a Hawthorne. And if Poe were alive, he would not have to invent horror; horror would invent him." Horror invented Richard Wright, and *Native Son* exposes the "demonic city" at the heart of American civilization.

The trial scene particularly characterizes Wright's concern for society. He pits Max against Buckley, as true and false prophets, engaged in a verbal battle concerning not only Bigger's life but also the welfare of the city. The debate is not, as some critics complain, a mere rehash of the novel's themes, but an exciting dialectical argument reminiscent again of *Paradise Lost.*

The trial is seen as a ritualized event designed to protect the city from the forces of evil. It is clear from the time of the inquest that "evil" has already been defined. The evidence Buckley brought against Bigger then was supposed "to make white men and women feel that nothing short of a quick blotting out of his life would make the city safe again." Later, as State's Attorney for the people in the courtroom, Buckley confirms them in their self-righteousness. Sounding like an Old Testament prophet, he warns them that there is a beast in the city, that the city must destroy the beast if the social fabric is to remain whole. His language is biblical. Bigger is depicted as a "maddened ape," "a rapacious beast" who has left his den. Every decent human being should want to "crush with his heel the woolly head of this black lizard, to keep him from scuttling on his belly farther over the earth and spitting forth his venom of death." Buckley ends his oration to the jury by urging its members to tell the people that, in the city, "jungle law does not prevail."

Max's speech contains the same imagery: there *is* a beast in the city, he argues, but the beast is *in us.* In keeping with the mission of the true prophet, Max tries to awaken the people to their responsibility for the evil they are suffering. The continuing oppression of the Negro has placed a corpse in our midst, Max says: "It has made itself a home in the wild forest of our great cities, amid the rank and choking vegetation of our slums! It has forgotten our language! In order to live it has sharpened its claws! It has grown hard and calloused! It has developed a capacity for hate and fury which we cannot understand! . . . By night it creeps from its lair and steals toward the settlements of civilization! And at the sight of a kind face it does not lie down upon its back and kick up its heels playfully to be tickled and stroked. No; it leaps to kill!" By denying the black man a place in their civilization they have threatened their own lives. Max presents an apocalyptic vision to the jury: the city will die if its citizens do not act to remove the evil they themselves have created. If Max seems a tragic figure at the end of *Native Son,* so does America.

Urban Racism Causes Bigger's Irrationality

Seodial Deena

Seodial Deena, a doctoral candidate in literature and criticism at Indiana University of Pennsylvania, discusses how the racist setting of *Native Son* causes Bigger to behave irrationally. Bigger senses that his fate is already determined by the segregation of blacks in Chicago. He fears the conflict between the races and expresses that fear through the violence he has learned in the black community. Finally, Bigger revolts in an attempt to fulfill his fantasies about the glittering city of the newspapers and movies, but he remains a victim of city politics and the media, which both condemn him as a beast.

According to Lola Jones Amis, Ralph Ellison declares in *Shadow and Act* that in Richard Wright's fiction, the Negro has one of three roles. He can be passive, as the Southern whites would like him to be, and resolve his personal conflicts in religion, or he can establish his own middle-class society and become the white man's accomplice in oppression, or he can reject the entire Southern social system and assume the role of a criminal, which will cause physical violence. According to Wright in "How Bigger Was Born," most blacks would choose the first two roles. Only the Bigger Thomases would choose the last, and indeed Bigger Thomas does choose the last role.

Why does Bigger revolt in such an irrational manner? Why kill Mary Dalton? Why perform such brutal acts as cutting off her head and burning her body? Why crush Bessie's head with a stone and throw her body down the chimney? Michel Fabre quotes Burton Rascoe's response to these questions:

> When I carefully examine all the evidences Mr. Wright offers to prove that Bigger Thomas should have become a murderer and that the guilt lies on our heads, I remain emphatically

Excerpted from "The Irrationality of Bigger Thomas's World: A Frightening View for the Twenty-First Century Urban Population," by Seodial Deena, *College Language Association Journal*, vol. 38, no. 1, 1994. Reprinted with permission from the *College Language Association Journal*.

unconvinced. I can't see that Bigger Thomas had anything more to contend with, in childhood or youth, than I had or dozens of my friends had. Their lives and mine have not been velvety, but we do not want to kill people because of this.

This approach by Rascoe is very naive and idealistic about Bigger's dilemma. One may never be able to justify Bigger's criminal actions, but their motivations can be cited as the irrationality of Bigger's world. In this essay, I shall endeavor to show that the society that molds Bigger Thomas kills him, but before it kills him, it twists him and makes him a killer.

THE CONFLICT BETWEEN BLACK AND WHITE

The irrationality of Bigger's world comes from the conflict between the white world and the black world. Wright explains why he created such a fictional world in which he placed Bigger.

> There are two worlds, the white world and the black world, and they are physically separated. There are white schools and black schools, white churches and black churches, white businesses and black businesses, white graveyards and black graveyards, and, for all I know, a white God and a black God.

Bigger's world is vividly depicted in the first scene of the novel. The setting is a one-room, rat-infested apartment, where there is limited privacy, and the confines of the walls reflect the narrowness and limitation of opportunities of Bigger's world. In this world there is fear, shame, insecurity, struggle for survival, violence, and death. The huge, black rat, filled with fear, strikes back at Bigger when he threatens the rat's existence. As Bigger lifts the skillet to strike the rat and Buddy blocks the hole with the box, the fate of the rat is determined. There is no hope, and escape becomes futile. This scene foreshadows the brief existence of Bigger in his confined world. He is filled with fear, shame, and violence. His hope for survival or escape is futile, his hole is blocked, and his fate is already determined by the laws of the white world.

Bigger is filled with shame because the white world makes him feel that he is not equal to the white man. His remark that he could fly a plane if he had a chance brings laughter from Gus. Yet Gus agrees that if Bigger were not black, if Bigger had money, if the whites let him go to aviation school, Bigger could fly a plane. These "ifs" demonstrate that Bigger's world lacks the things that the white world has.

The white world has plenty of food, comfort, privacy, opportunities, money, and fun. Bigger wants to experience this world, but he is not allowed to enter it, so he is filled with hostility. The movies, the press, the rules, the people, and all that make up the system clearly tell him that he cannot enter the white world. The fearful, black rat represents his world, and the confident, white cat represents the white world. The two do not fellowship with each other. If they do, the black rat will be devoured by the white cat.

Furthermore, people like Jan, Mary, Mr. and Mrs. Dalton, and Peggy unconsciously make him feel ashamed of his world.

> He was very conscious of his black skin and there was in him a prodding conviction that Jan and men like him had made it so that he would be conscious of that black skin. Did not white people despise a black skin? Then why was Jan doing this? Why was Mary standing there so eagerly, with shining eyes? What could they get out of this? Maybe they did not despise him? But they made him feel his black skin by just standing there looking at him, one holding his hand and the other smiling. He felt he had no physical existence at all right then; he was something he hated, the badge of shame which he knew was attached to a black skin. It was a shadowy region, a No Man's Land, the ground that separated the white world from the black that he stood upon.

BIGGER'S FEAR LEADS TO VIOLENCE

Bigger is filled with fear because he knows that the white world is ready to devour him. This is why he and his friends rob only the black folks, and the idea of robbing the first white man, Blums, scares him. James A. Miller points out that in the white man's world, Bigger is inarticulate. He claims that Bigger is afraid to speak, and when he speaks it is in the form of short answers such as "yessum," "nawsah," "no mam," and "yes mam." Even at home he does not speak much, but he feels a sense of rage because the power and influence of the white world are present. For example, the little shack of an apartment is controlled by Mr. Dalton, and Bigger's mother and sister pressure him to work for Mr. Dalton. Vera and her mother become instruments of the white world since they will fall into Ellison's second category. They want to escape this world to go into middle-class society. Buddy is probably no better. He is passive, and he accepts the white world. When Bigger gets the chauffeur job with the Daltons, Buddy remarks, "You got a good job now. You can get a better gal than Bessie." But Bigger's sharp insight penetrates the blindness of his family. He continually refers to Vera and Buddy as being blind to the real things that matter in life.

However, in the gang or street world Bigger is very articulate. He converses freely. He gives orders to Jack, Gus, and G.H. in the poolroom. He speaks freely to Bessie. He shares with her his plan of demanding ransom money from the Daltons. Bigger is confident in these worlds because they are removed from the influence of the white world. In these worlds he gives the orders, whereas in the white world of the car, the Daltons' house, and the court, he is given the orders. In fact, he is so afraid of the white world that he takes his gun and knife with him. These weapons make him feel equal to the white man.

VIOLENCE BEGETS VIOLENCE

Bigger's world is filled with violence, especially violence toward the society that represses his chance of becoming a man. This is the society that has murdered his father in the South. This is the society that lynches black men, and which, according to Wright's introduction, picks up the first black boy seen in the streets for a crime he knows nothing about. Bigger himself has been picked up in a similar manner and sent to reform school. Bigger tells Mr. Dalton: "They said I was stealing. But I wasn't. . . . I was with some boys and the police picked us up."

According to Robert James Butler, since the appearance of the novel, critics have raised questions about its heavy preoccupation with violence. Malcolm Cowley worried about the author's use of violence. David Daiches complained that the novel's thesis is seriously destroyed because the killing of Mary Dalton is so "violent and unusual." Twenty-one years later, James Baldwin argued that the greatest criticism against the novel is Wright's "gratuitous and compulsive" interest in violence in the book. He claims that the root of the violence is never examined. Echoing Baldwin, Nathan Scott complained in 1970 that Wright is obsessed with violence and that this obsession forces him to destroy his characters. However, in 1986 Robert James Butler demonstrated that Wright was always in control of the violence, and that "*Native Son*, his masterwork, uses violence extensively but as a necessary and powerful reflector of the deepest recesses of its central character's radically divided nature."

When the society creates such a "radically divided nature" in Bigger Thomas, then the manifestation of such a character is irrationality, and the products of such irrationality are shame, fear, and violence. This violence, from beginning to end, becomes a violent protest against a system that alienates Bigger. In a sense, Mary also faces alienation. She wants to know more of the rougher side of life, more of Bigger and his people, and more of the struggles of humanity, but her white skin and her rich social class alienate her from such experiences. On the other hand, Bigger wants to experience the rich and luxurious white world, but his black skin and poor social class alienate him from these experiences. Mary responds to this alienation by trying to reach out to Bigger's world, without realizing the shame and embarrassment she is causing him. Bigger explains to Max, "She made me feel like a dog. I was so mad I wanted to cry. . . ." On the other hand, Bigger reacts with irrational crimes, which are filled with shame, fear, and violence. Max explains to Bigger, "Bigger you should have tried to understand. She was acting toward you only as she knew how." To this Bigger replies, "Well, I acted toward her only as I knew how."

THE GULF BETWEEN BLACK AND WHITE IN CHICAGO

Mary, Jan, Mr. and Mrs. Dalton, and Max are all pawns of the system. They think that their efforts to bridge the gap between the white world and black world are serious, but their efforts are games they do not even realize they are playing. Mary feels that by eating soul food, drinking at "colored places," and singing "Swing Low, Sweet Chariot," she can experience the black world. Mr. and Mrs. Dalton feel that by giving over five million dollars to colored schools, giving Bigger a job, and being reasonable employers to Bigger they are helping the black world. Jan and Max feel that by using the communist's idea of brotherhood and the political rhetoric of black representation, they can solve the problems created by the system. What they do not realize, but what Bigger sees, is that Bigger's world is like black hell and that their world is like the bright heaven. And after years of torment, privation, and segregation in his black world or hell, he is unable to act rationally. Furthermore, even if Bigger, like the rich man in hell, cries out for help and deliverance, he cannot be delivered because the system says that there is a great gulf between the two worlds.

Although I disagree with Charles W. Scruggs's view that the conclusion of the novel is flawed, he provides great insight into the role of the city in *Native Son*. Scruggs claims that the novel's real theme is "man's need for human community." He further claims that the city has failed to provide this "human community" because it is a "closed society" which disregards Bigger and his people as human beings, "shoves them from sight, herds them into a carefully defined space, and then ignores them." This is the city to which Bigger becomes a victim.

In the introduction, "How Bigger Was Born," Wright justifies the use of Chicago as the setting.

> The urban environment of Chicago, offering a more stimulating life, made the Negro Bigger Thomases react more violently than even in the South. More than ever I began to see and understand the environmental factors which made for this extreme condition. It was not that Chicago segregated Negroes more than the South, but that Chicago had more to offer, that Chicago's physical aspect—noisy, crowded, filled with the sense of power and fulfillment—did so much more to dazzle the mind with a taunting sense of possible achievement that the segregation it did impose brought forth from Bigger a reaction more obstreperous than in the South.

Indeed the Chicago environment is unique and suitable to justify Bigger's violent and irrational revolt. New York and London are older cities. They have had longer lives to balance materialistic aspects with cultural values, yet they are not balanced. Even so, Chicago, a fast-growing city of industry and commerce, lacks this balance. Materialism dominates its culture and leaves Bigger Thomas in a spiritually dead environment. Furthermore, it is "a city of extremes; torrid summers and sub-zero winters; a city which has become the pivot of the Eastern, Western, Northern, and Southern poles of the nation." These extremes are reflected in the rich and poor and in the black and white.

FANTASIES OF THE CITY CAUSE BIGGER'S REVOLT

As a result of these factors, the city estranges Bigger Thomas from the religion and culture of his mother and his people. His real life exists on the streets of the city, with Gus, G.H., and Jack playing pool, smoking, drinking, and robbing. Gradually Bigger slips away from religion, and the environment leaves him with no spiritual or cultural sustenance. It desensitizes him and leaves him to roam the streets. It also molds him into a twisted, irrational killer, then condemns him. When he realizes his fate, that he is going to be executed, and that he needs spiritual help, he is unable to respond positively. He rejects Reverend Hammond, his mother's pastor. He fears and hates the preacher who tells him "to bow down and ask for a mercy he knows he needs, but his pride would not let him bow down." Nor will this alienation from religion let him listen to his mother's plea for him to pray. Yet as he deceptively assures his mother, "I'll pray, Ma," "something screams deep down in him that it is a lie."

Bigger also revolts with irrationality because he is trying to react to and answer the call of the city glitters and fantasies. These glitters and fantasies reach his mind by means of the newspapers, magazines, radios, and movies. For example, Bigger and Jack visit the Regal Theater to view the movies *The Gay Woman* and *Trader Horn*. Apart from depicting an ugly black world and a beautiful white world, the movies arouse their fantasies. Bigger wonders if Mr. Dalton is rich like the white man in *The Gay Woman*. He further fantasizes whether Mr. Dalton has a daughter who is a hot kind of girl and who may give him money to keep her secrets. These are some of the glittering motivations behind Bigger's acceptance of the job.

Bigger Thomas takes a job as a chauffeur for the Daltons, and almost immediately his glitter-fantasy seems real. But "not all that glitters is gold." Bigger discovers that Mr. Dalton is rich, that he has a daughter, and that she has a clandestine affair. She confides in him, but instead of getting a secret romantic relationship with her or large sums of money, he becomes her murderer and lives in further fear. Furthermore, the glittering city culture pushes him to try for ransom money of ten thousand dollars, but reality stings him. He is caught, imprisoned, tried, found guilty, and executed. . . .

THE POLITICS OF SURVIVAL IN THE CITY

Like Richard Wright, Bigger Thomas comes from the South with dreams of prosperity in Chicago, but he lacks the skills necessary for survival in the city. He lives with his mother, his sister Vera, and his brother Buddy in a one-room apartment. The naggings and negative predictions of an ambitious, poverty-stricken, and hard-working mother drive him from the crowded room to the street-life of movies, robberies, and gangs. His hopes are shattered, he becomes a victim of the city, and he finds himself caught up by forces outside his understanding and control.

Two other factors that aid the system and city to create irrationality in Bigger Thomas' world are self-centered politicians like Buckley and a vicious and influential media. Buckley, the state's attorney, is white, brutal, and merciless. There is no grace in him, and Max's hope for Bigger's freedom is shattered as Buckley hurries the case for Bigger's execution. Buckley uses fourteen pressmen as witnesses, and while he uses the press to influence the crowd to press for Bigger's execution, he also uses Bigger's execution to campaign for his personal, political reelection to the post of state attorney.

Buckley visits Bigger in his cell and pretends to befriend him: "Buckley led Bigger to a window through which he looked and saw the streets below crowded with masses of people in all directions. 'See that, boy? Those people would like to lynch you. That's why I am asking you to trust me and talk to me. The quicker we get this thing over, the better for you.'" But the reader knows that the quickness of the case is advantageous not for Bigger but for Buckley, who uses the rhetoric of Western metaphysics to cover up his selfish and corrupt motives. He also uses the crowd to intimidate Bigger to confess so that he can get Bigger condemned and executed, thus using Bigger's fate to motivate the people to vote for him.

Such a debased system is represented in the character of Buckley, whose campaign poster says, "IF YOU BREAK THE LAW, YOU CAN'T WIN." But Bigger also knows that if you do not break the law, you keep losing. Therefore, politicians such as Buckley continue to produce, with their selfish rhetoric, a high degree of irrationality in the Bigger Thomases of today.

The media produces a deadening effect on Bigger. It is closely interwoven with politics and politicians, and it displays that lustful hunger for news, despite the consequences. This is how Bigger's perceptive eyes view the pressmen:

> They were not rich and distant like Mr. Dalton, and they were harder than Britten, but in a more impersonal way, a way that maybe was more dangerous than Britten's. Back and forth they walked across the basement floor in the glare of the furnace with their hats on and cigars and cigarettes in their mouths. Bigger felt in them a coldness that disregarded everybody. They seemed like men out for keen sport.

In fact the pressmen are so corrupt that they would give

bribes for information. As one of the men places "a slender wad of paper" in Bigger's hand, he whispers, "Keep still. It's for you. I want you to give me the dope."

Once the death of Mary Dalton is linked to Bigger Thomas, the press continually renders reports that are filled with racial-stereotypical images and phrases. These reports link Bigger Thomas's crime of murder with rape. As Bigger rereads the line "AUTHORITIES HINT SEX CRIME," he realizes that "[t]o hint that he had committed a sex crime was to pronounce the death sentence; it meant a wiping out of his life even before he was captured." He becomes aware of his hopeless fate in the hands of the law, politics, and press, for he perceptively observes how the press has incited the audience to demand his execution. Furthermore, after the press has portrayed him as a "sex-slayer," "ape," "a jungle beast," and "a beast utterly untouched by the softening influences of modern civilization," it is only rational that the crowd would shout: "Lynch 'im! Kill 'im."

CHAPTER 4

Religion, Racism, and Violence: Themes in *Native Son*

READINGS ON
NATIVE SON

Native Son Is a Novel of Religious Skepticism

Robert L. Douglas

Robert L. Douglas is Associate Professor of art history and pan-African studies at the University of Louisville, Kentucky. Douglas notes that Wright portrays Reverend Hammond in *Native Son* as deferential toward whites. Bigger thus becomes skeptical about religion as his own preacher is meekly suppliant toward God while he lets himself be beaten by society. Out of frustration and cynicism, Bigger abandons religion as an instrument for social change, thus establishing the theme of religious doubt in the novel.

The role of religion in the lives of black people has occasioned some of the most celebrated discussions and debates since blacks became a part of American society. In spite of the fact that slave owners had instructed blacks in a strict Christian doctrine, some anomalies took place in the Christian practice of black people. Not only did the African slaves have their own peculiar ideas about how the deity should be worshipped, but they also wove religious ritual, ceremony, and incantations into the daily fabric of their lives. While these anomalies—once labelled primitive by E. Franklin Frazier and others—are now known to be religious syncretism encompassing African religious phenomena, the masses of blacks have made these practices part of their religious tradition. Therefore, any writing which attempts to portray black life must present some aspect of their particular religious practices. The writings of Richard Wright are no exception.

Since Wright was the first Afro-American writer to spark my interest with his religious allusions, I would like to discuss his use of religious elements in . . . *Native Son*. The [two] aspects of black religious life portrayed by Wright and

Excerpted from "Religious Orthodoxy and Skepticism in Richard Wright's *Uncle Tom's Children* and *Native Son*," by Robert L. Douglas, in *Richard Wright: Myths and Realities,* edited by C. James Trotman (New York: Garland, 1988). Reprinted with permission from the author.

the focus of this inquiry are: (1) the treatment of the minister; (2) the concept of religion or religious worldview. . . .

REV. HAMMOND IS WEAK IN THE FACE OF WHITES

Rev. Hammond in *Native Son* is condescending and supplicating. Rev. Hammond offers Bigger's mother a theology steeped in suffering and endurance. He believes that man must pay for the original sins of Adam and Eve. He also believes that Adam had begged for forgiveness, and the tenor of his advice to Bigger is that Bigger should do no less. Bigger should not only beg for forgiveness for his violent acts, but he should also do as Rev. Hammond asks: "Son, promise me yuh'll stop hatin' long enuff for Gawd's love to come inter yo heart." Rev. Hammond's meek attitude toward God is manifested in his deference toward whites. When Jan enters the room where Bigger is allowed to receive visitors, Rev. Hammond "took a step backwards, bowed, and said 'Good mawnin' suh.'" He condescends to a man that is half his age. Rev. Hammond acts in this manner, no doubt, because Jan is white and Rev. Hammond accepts his own inferior social position.

Wright continues his portrayal of Rev. Hammond in *Native Son* as a meager, obsequious and self-effacing individual. Wright tells his reader that in the presence of Mr. Dalton, "The preacher came forward slowly, hat in hand" and that he proceeded to ingratiate himself. After stating how "sorrowful" he was over Mary Dalton's death, Rev. Hammond supplicates, "Ah knows of yo good work, suh, 'n the likes of this shouldn't come t'yuh.". . .

Rev. Hammond is weak and ingratiating, beaten by societal forces. All of his energy is directed at saving souls at the expense of the bodies and earthly comforts. Wright, therefore, clothes his skepticism of certain religious beliefs and practices, especially as they pertain to Blacks, in the feelings and attitudes of his protagonist, Bigger.

Although the treatment of the minister types by Wright is individually different, no doubt as types, they share similar characteristics with ministers who are not black. A more distinctive picture of the black minister might have shown his pulpit dramatics or described rhythmic and poetic sermons—none of which appears in [*Native Son*]. . . .

At the root of the religious worldview of the black masses is the perception of God in the most elemental and literal levels. Such practices are often characterized as child-like and unsophisticated. Dr. Benjamin E. Mays in his classic study, *The Negro's God as Reflected in His Literature*, demonstrated that blacks' belief in God assumes an orthodox point of view from an Old Testament orientation. Mays also contends that blacks place special emphasis upon "the magical, spectral, partial, revengeful and anthropomorphic nature of God."

Dr. Mays says that the black religious worldview is "compensatory when used or developed to support a shallow pragmatism." A religious belief becomes true when it satisfies a desire, if it uplifts and consoles even though the belief does not fit observed facts. Mays explains these assertions by saying:

> A dependent mother who prays to [God] twice daily asking him to bless her sons, preserve their lives, and cause them to prosper (thinking her task is done after she prays) is typical of an idea of God that supports such pragmatism.

As an example of the religious anomalies of blacks, such a worldview influences the mother's behavior: "it leads her to pray; it helps her to feel better; it saves her from worry, and it enables her to sleep at night.". . .

Dr. Mays states that the black view of God as it is reflected through black literature can be divided into three categories and time periods. The first, the other-worldly or the orthodox treatment with its compensatory pragmatism, appeared during slavery. The second, God's concern for black social and psychological needs, can be placed between the failure of Reconstruction and the First World War. The third, the tendency to abandon the idea of God as a useful agent of social change, appears more often in black literature after the First World War. Dr. Mays contends that this disillusionment was caused by the fact that the promise of greater social freedom did not materialize as many hoped following the War. According to Dr. Mays none of the three religious views ever existed solely by itself, and although his study does not go beyond 1937, much about this theory remains relevant. The skepticism and cynicism evident in Wright may be seen as falling into Mays' third category. To quote Dr. Mays, "for recent writers to consider the idea of God as useless is an effort to reconstruct the world socially."

BIGGER BECOMES AN ATHEIST

In *Native Son*, Wright shows religious doubt, frustration, and cynicism in a most blatant manner as Wright's protagonist expresses the frustration born out of waiting for God to solve his problem. When Max questions Bigger about his religious beliefs, Bigger tells him, "I didn't like it. There was nothing in it." Bigger feels that "churchgoing" is a delusion and a way for keeping poor people happy while they remain poor. He expresses his doubts about church and the promises of religion.

> Aw, all they did was sing and shout and pray all the time. And it didn't get 'em nothing. All the colored folks do that, but it don't get 'em nothing. The white folks got everything.

Bigger also states that he never felt happy in church nor did he want to be because "nothing but poor folks get happy in church." Bigger's skepticism about the social value of church borders on an astute political awareness. He refuses to be caught up in the traditional religious orthodoxy of the heaven-or-hell alternative or the idea that one would receive a reward for his suffering after his death. He says,

> I want to be happy in this world, not out of it. I didn't want that kind of happiness. The white folks like for us to be religious, then they can do what they want to with us.

If Dr. Mays is correct that the black tends to move beyond God as a catalytic social agent and that black writers reflect this change through their art, then Wright's skepticism and his incipient agnosticism blossom in his characterization of Bigger Thomas. In fact, Bigger is portrayed as a developing atheist. The more Rev. Hammond attempts to awaken in Bigger a sense of guilt and forgiveness, the more Bigger rejects the preacher and his theology. Later, as Rev. Hammond tries to assure Bigger that he would meet his mother in the "great bye and bye," Bigger's atheistic feelings became more evident. The reader is told that, "Something screamed deep down in [Bigger] that it was a lie, that seeing [his mother] after they killed him would never be." After listening to Rev. Hammond's orthodox view of creation—man's sinful place in it and how Jesus was sent to save man—Bigger thought about how "he had killed within himself the preacher's haunting picture of life even before he had killed Mary." Also, Bigger felt that "to those who wanted to kill him he was not human, not included in that picture of creation."

Wright prepares his reader for Bigger's involvement with the death of Mary Dalton and Bessie as well as the inevitable consequences by showing the reader the brutality of the life that Bigger was forced to survive and the situations that fired Bigger's doubts. After allowing Rev. Hammond to put a cross around his neck, Bigger comes out of the Dalton home, where he is taken for further questioning; and he sees a burning cross placed there by the Ku Klux Klan. His thoughts become an insight into his cynicism. "He had a cross of salvation round his throat and they were burning one to tell him that they hated him." Bigger felt that he had been trapped by the preacher who was also trapped in a religion that could not save either of them.

A Missed Clue Proves the Existence of Racism in *Native Son*

Doyle W. Walls

Doyle W. Walls of the University of Wisconsin-Madison explains that Bigger's ransom note should have failed to convince authorities of its legitimacy because of a vital linguistic clue that clearly points to an African American as the killer. Walls argues that racist police and prosecutors dismiss Bigger as less than human and incapable of deliberate action, and thus miss the clue.

In his *Black Boy,* Richard Wright relates the story of a forged note he wrote at the age of eighteen in order to check out books at a library in Memphis. Wright told the white man whose library card he was using what he was planning to do. He would forge a note to make it appear that the white man was making the request: "I finally wrote what I thought would be a foolproof note: *Dear Madam: Will you please let this nigger boy*—I used the word 'nigger' to make the librarian feel that I could not possibly be the author of the note—*have some books by H.L. Mencken?* I forged the white man's name."

A MATTER OF LINGUISTICS

Wright's fictional creation, the twenty-year-old Bigger Thomas of *Native Son,* also forges a white man's name to a note he has written. This note, however, is a ransom note concerning Mary Dalton, a young woman whom Bigger has already killed. Just before he forges the name *"Red"*—which is meant to turn everyone's attention to Jan Erlone, the communist—Bigger writes, *"Do what this letter say."* While there is certainly little similarity between the intellectual capacity of Wright at eighteen and his protagonist, one can not help noticing that Wright's forged note shows an awareness of the "typical" white man's diction, while Bigger's note fails—that is, should have failed as a forgery—in one important respect concerning the grammar of the ruling class.

Although it is only the absence of one letter required by Standard American English that constitutes the piece of evidence that could point to the murderer, the clue looms large on the page. The legibility of Bigger's handwriting is not at issue: "He should disguise his handwriting. He changed the pencil from his right to his left hand. He would not write it; he would print it . . . he printed slowly in big round letters." With Mary Dalton dead, the authorities' two principal suspects, after questioning Bigger, are Jan Erlone and Bigger himself. No matter how the note was signed, it seems obvious that the authorities would realize that Bigger's vernacular, not Jan's, would produce, "*Do what this letter say.*"

Wright, responding to an article which was critical of his novel, wrote: "If there had been *one* person in the Dalton household who viewed Bigger Thomas as a human being, the crime would have been solved in half an hour. Did not Bigger himself know that it was the denial of his personality that enabled him to escape detection so long? The one piece of incriminating evidence which would have solved the 'murder mystery' was Bigger's humanity, and the Daltons, Britten, and the newspaper men could not see or admit the living clue of Bigger's humanity under their very eyes!" Although Wright is arguing the larger issue of Bigger's humanity, his word choice also intimates that a reading based on conventions of the detective story might well be profitable. One learns from *Black Boy* that when Wright first began to read he was interested in mysteries and that his reading included *Flynn's Detective Weekly*. . . . Robert Felgar notes, in a discussion of *The Outsider* and *Native Son,* "how much Wright's fiction owes to the conventions of the detective story."

John G. Cawelti mentions "crime and clues" as one of the six primary elements in the pattern of the classical detective story and writes of their "paradoxical relationship": "First, the crime must be surrounded by a number of tangible clues that make it absolutely clear that some agency is responsible for it, and, second, it must appear to be insoluble." Although pieces of Mary's bones would later be found in the furnace as well as one of her earrings, the first and only clue until that time which points to criminal activity is the ransom note composed by Bigger. Yet when the bones and earring are discovered, Bigger is standing among the men near the furnace. A paradox exists, but it is not the paradox which Cawelti mentions in his discussion of the classical detective story. Wright's paradox is ironic. He has spelled out a tangible clue; however, rather than making the crime seem "insoluble," the paradox is that no one sees the obvious.

Having overlooked a piece of solid evidence, the prosecution turns to what the reader realizes is ludicrous, trumped-up "evidence": "Five white men came to the stand and said that the handwriting on the kidnap note was his; that it was the same writing which they had found on his 'homework papers taken from the files of the school he used to attend.'" Bigger's conscious attempt to disguise his handwriting by switching the pencil to his left hand could not, it seems, deter these specialists! Having failed to read the sign of Bigger's identity, the five white men do appear to find one clue: the authorities intend to have Bigger Thomas convicted one way or another, with or without legitimate evidence.

THE WHITE COPS FAIL INTELLECTUALLY AND MORALLY

The instance of black vernacular in Bigger's ransom note is no linguistic error; it is a direct transcription of the Black English Vernacular that he speaks. However, Bigger's use of BEV in this particular situation can be considered an "error" when read in conjunction with the conventions of the detective story: his error would have been—had it been discovered—that he slipped up in trying to mask himself linguistically. J.L. Dillard records that Black English differs most from the dialects of white Americans in "the system of its verbs." The white authorities fail to read one of the most blatant of linguistic clues on two levels: intellectual and moral.

Since the white men had received educational opportunities denied to Bigger on the basis of race and since their linguistic environment would increase the possibility of their detecting Bigger's deviation from Standard American English, they fail on an intellectual level. Beyond their lack of sensitivity to language and their deficient detective skills, the authorities are morally culpable for their prejudice that prevents them from understanding that Bigger Thomas is a human being with a potential for action beyond their limited perception of him.

Their failure helps Wright illuminate a mystery of race relations: that the white men did not know Bigger's language tells the reader that they did not know him. Bigger makes this complaint to Max, his attorney: "White folks and black folks is strangers. We don't know what each other is thinking." What avenue could be more telling toward discovering who a person is than that person's language? In a small and concrete sense, the authorities overlook the clue which they could have used for their own limited ends to solve the mystery of Mary Dalton's murder. In a larger sense, they overlook a clue concerning Bigger's humanity. The failure of the authorities to read that clue is evidence of their guilt in race relations and, ultimately, the guilt which they share in Mary Dalton's murder.

Native Son Is a Novel of Revolt

Steven J. Rubin

Literature scholar Steven J. Rubin of the University of South Florida explores the theme of personal revolt in *Native Son.* Bigger's revolt, he claims, grows out of hatred and fear. He is an alienated man struggling against a corrupt system, and his act of murder is the most meaningful moment in his life. Only through revolt, through violence, does Bigger feel free.

The early fiction of Richard Wright, comprised of short stories written in the thirties and culminating in *Native Son* (1940), is primarily an expression of personal outrage and frustration. Although Wright's literary heritage has been traced to the American Naturalists, recent readings of his works suggest that Wright was not as confined by that tradition as has generally been believed. Working within the framework of social protest, Wright probed other more metaphysical issues, which were later to become of even greater importance to him. In dramatizing the plight of each of his heroes, from Big Boy in "Big Boy Leaves Home," to Bigger Thomas in *Native Son,* Wright explored the motivating forces behind their actions. As their personal dramas unfolded, he developed such themes as the possibility of freedom, man's isolation and alienation, the inherent irrationality of modern American society, and the nature and form of personal rebellion within that society.

Native Son is, as Edward Margolies in *The Art of Richard Wright* points out, as much a psychological novel with clear existential implications, as it is sociological. Bigger Thomas is not only a Black man struggling against an oppressive white society, but also Wright's archetypal rebel, desperately seeking recognition and meaning within a world that has offered him none. Alienated from the mainstream of society

Excerpted from "Richard Wright and Albert Camus: The Literature of Revolt," by Steven J. Rubin, *International Fiction Review,* vol. 8, no. 1, 1981. Reprinted with permission from *International Fiction Review.*

and betrayed by his own environment, Bigger, like Wright's earlier heroes, searches for an effective means of vanquishing his personal sense of worthlessness. Ironically, like the protagonists of *Uncle Tom's Children,* Bigger's revolt is simultaneously victorious and self-destructive.

The literature of revolt is born from the recognition on the part of many modern writers that meaning and purpose are not an integral part of the universe in which man finds himself. *Native Son,* written at a time when Wright was preoccupied with social issues, also represents an examination of the nature of personal rebellion, a theme which dominated much of the thinking of such modern European writers as André Malraux, Jean-Paul Sartre, and especially Albert Camus. . . .

In Wright's first volume of short stories, *Uncle Tom's Children* (1938), physical rebellion becomes the dominant theme and the means by which his characters achieve freedom and identity. Wright's early heroes seek fulfillment of their personality and a purpose to their otherwise meaningless existence through violent action. In similar fashion, Bigger Thomas, confused and alone, can find no conventional way to bridge the gap between his aspirations and the reality of his condition. In "How Bigger was Born," Wright explained the need for rebellion: "In *Native Son* I tried to show that man, bereft of a culture and unanchored by property, can travel but one path if he reacts positively, but unthinkingly to the prizes and goals of civilization; and that path is emotionally blind rebellion."

REVOLT OUT OF HATRED AND FEAR

As the novel opens, Bigger is seen as a man conditioned by hatred and a sense of racial exclusion: "I just can't get used to it," Bigger said. "I swear to God I can't, I know I oughtn't think about it, but I can't help it. Everytime I think about it I feel like somebody's poking a red-hot iron down my throat. God-dammit, look! We live here and they live there. We black and they white. They got things and we ain't. They do things and we can't. It's just like living in jail. Half the time I feel like I'm on the outside of the world peeping in through a knot-hole in the fence." Throughout Book I, "Fear," Bigger is portrayed as a man in conflict, not only with white society, but also with his surroundings, his family, his peers, and ultimately with himself. Bigger is not able to escape the sordidness of his condition through religion, as does his mother, or through alcohol, as does his mistress Bessie. For him there are no external evasions, and as his anxiety and frustration mount Bigger begins to feel a sense of impending disaster: "Bigger felt an urgent need to hide his growing and deepening feeling of hysteria; he had to get rid of it or else he would succumb to it . . . his self-trust was gone. Confidence could only come again now through action so violent that it would make him forget."

Bigger takes a job as a chauffeur for the Daltons, a wealthy white philanthropic family who support the NAACP but are nevertheless one of the city's biggest slum landlords. Through a strange series of circumstances Bigger, in a moment of fear and panic, kills their daughter Mary. The murder, although ostensibly a mistake, is an accident only in the narrowest sense, for Bigger has long dreamed of such an act. The full meaning of his crime does not become clear to him until after the murder, but he had long had a foreboding of such violence: "I feel like something awful's going to happen to me. . . . Naw, it ain't like something going to happen to me. It's . . . It's like I was going to do something I can't help." Bigger fantasizes about destruction, of dropping bombs on the white world, and in one rare moment of insight even admits to the possibility of murder as an antidote to his extreme anguish and despair: "He knew that the moment he allowed what his life meant to enter fully into his consciousness, he would either kill himself or someone else."

Bigger's killing of Mary becomes the one meaningful act of his life, giving him a new sense of freedom and identity and a capacity for action on a grand scale. Up to this time Bigger has cowered in fear before the white world. Now, as he plots his next move, the many options that are opened give him a new sense of power and possibility: "He lay again on the bed, his mind whirling with images born of a multitude of impulses. He could run away; he could remain; he could even go down and confess what he had done. The mere thought that these avenues of action were open to him made him feel free, that his life was his, that he held his future in his hands."

Out of apparent fear of betrayal, Bigger brutally slays his mistress Bessie. These two acts place him irrevocably outside the social order of all men, both white and black. Unlike his killing of Mary, the murder of Bessie is neither accidental nor truly necessary for his protection. It is simply proof of his new ability to act. Although Bigger is afraid he will be overwhelmed by a feeling of guilt, this second murder, like the first, gives him a sense of liberation and an even greater control over his destiny: "In all of his life these two murders were the most meaningful things that had ever happened to him. He was living, truly and deeply. . . . Never had he had the chance to live out the consequences of his actions; never had his will been so free as in this night and day of fear and murder and flight."

Bigger is finally discovered to be the murderer and is captured after a search of the entire Black section of Chicago. Max, a white Communist Party lawyer, becomes his attorney and presents an impassioned plea, linking Bigger's deviant actions to his environment and the transgressions of a prejudiced society. Privately, however, Max, whose thinking does not go beyond sociological explanations, is somewhat bewildered as to Bigger's true motivation. Bigger tries to explain that his action has made him understand himself as a man: "What I killed for I *am*! . . . What I killed for must've been good! . . . When a man kills, it's for something. . . . I didn't know I was really alive in this world until I felt things hard enough to kill for 'em.". . .

BIGGER IS AN ALIENATED MAN STRUGGLING WITHIN THE SYSTEM

In the final pages of *Native Son*, Bigger Thomas, condemned to death, also attempts to understand the relationship between man and the absurdity of his environment. Rejecting the solace of religion, he is determined to die alone, as he has lived. In talking with Max, however, he realizes that other men have lived and felt as he has. He is finally able to send a belated gesture of fraternity to Jan, whose help Bigger has rejected throughout. As Max is leaving his cell for the last time, Bigger calls out to him: "Tell . . . Tell Mister . . . Tell Jan hello."

As his death approaches, Bigger . . . is free of fear of life and death. He has finally made peace with himself by realizing that his actions, although self-destructive, were the only possible responses to the series of injustices and irrationalities within his existence. As his execution nears, Bigger has no remorse; instead he is seen with "a faint, wry bitter smile.". . .

Bigger acts out of hatred, fear, and an innate longing to be free. Uneducated and inarticulate, he reacts unthinkingly to the underlying contradictions of an American society which proclaims the inherent worth of the individual and yet everywhere denies that worth to the Black man. . . . Bigger is not aware of the metaphysical implications of his protest. It is only after his action that he begins to experience a new knowledge of himself, his existence, and the nature of his surroundings. Directed immediately against the white majority, his rebellion eventually assumes a universal dimension and ultimately is . . . a protest against the entire scheme of things.

Native Son is as much a study of an alienated and lonely individual struggling to understand his existence, as it is an examination of racial prejudice and its effects. Bigger is forced into an alien existence because of the irrational and unjust nature of the society in which he lives. For Bigger, the opposite poles of aspiration and satisfaction can only be briefly united through violence. Murder becomes, paradoxically, the one creative act of his life: "He had murdered and had created a new life for himself.". . . Bigger is able to kill without remorse, for good and evil have become meaningless to him. Killing has become part of Bigger's definition of himself; and although Wright does not attempt to justify or condone murder, he does strive to explain the necessity of Bigger's actions. . . .

Wright clearly perceived the inconsistencies of the American system and tried to show, through Bigger Thomas, a man struggling within that system. Living in a society that had placed him next to obscurity, Bigger turns to violence as the only meaningful action open to him.

"What peculiar personality formation results," Wright later asked, "when millions of people are forced to live lives of outward submissiveness while trying to keep intact in their hearts a sense of worth of their own humanity." The answer, in part, is given by Wright in *Native Son*. Written in 1940, the novel gives an early indication of Wright's existential vision and the themes that were to preoccupy his thinking in the years to come.

Explaining the Violence of *Native Son*

Jerry H. Bryant

Jerry H. Bryant, author of *The Open Decision: The Contemporary American Novel and Its Intellectual Background,* examines the violence of *Native Son* and suggests that Bigger is a product of a newly violent world in which violence is both a national characteristic and a means of self-fulfillment. Bryant explains how Bigger's murder of Mary grows out of his need to save himself from a racist society. His violence gives his life worth; it empowers him and alleviates his fear, making him feel that only through violence is he really living.

Throughout his adult life, Richard Wright was preoccupied with the nature of a healthy society. He believed that only when people acknowledge each other's need for warmth, sympathy, and understanding can they build a social structure in which all can feel at home. These qualities were conspicuously absent for the black American of the 1930s, who, as Wright sees it, never felt at home in his own land. Certainly Bigger Thomas did not. Bigger is a representative black victim of white racism. More importantly, he is a representative modern man—at least one type of modern man. Closed off from self-fulfillment and self-expression, isolated from the world around him, he turns to violence, becoming, like his contemporaries of the same stamp, a threat to the civilization that produced him.

The murders that Bigger commits in *Native Son* break most of the rules of civilized behavior. Wright believes in those rules, and he does not allow us to applaud Bigger as an incipient revolutionary stoutly defending his manhood. Nor does Wright try morally to justify Bigger's actions. He presents them as reprehensible. Bigger smothers the white girl

Excerpted from "The Violence of *Native Son*," by Jerry H. Bryant, *Southern Review*, vol. 17, no. 2, 1981. Reprinted with permission from the author.

who tries, however clumsily, to befriend him, and then hacks her head off to fit her into the furnace to burn the evidence of his crime. He smashes the skull of his own black girlfriend after he has forced her to make love to him, and then throws her body down the air shaft of a deserted Chicago tenement, where the freezing night finishes her off. Both acts have an element of cowardice in them, committed against women who, physically weaker than Bigger, have entrusted themselves to his keeping. Both are connected directly or indirectly with Bigger's loveless appetite for sex— the white girl a forbidden object, the black girl one nobody cares about. Both acts are performed, at the most vulgar level, to save Bigger's skin, which he and his motives make us doubt is very much worth saving.

BIGGER'S NEED TO SAVE HIMSELF

Wright shows us how Bigger could do these things, the life he leads that produces so vicious a behavior. Bigger has been cramped by his environment, limited in his education, and prevented from developing his native understanding and sensibility. He can think only in the crudest terms and react only in the most basic ways. When Mary Dalton's blind mother enters her daughter's bedroom and nearly touches the terrified Bigger standing by the bed, his mind can handle only two alternatives—whether he will or will not get caught. To avoid getting caught, his slow mind finds only one course of action: to prevent Mary from rising up in her drunken stupor and speaking to Mrs. Dalton. But with an excess that characterizes most of his behavior, Bigger unintentionally kills her, becoming a perfect victim of a racist and capitalist environment.

During this scene, Bigger's behavior seems out of proportion to the apparent danger. It is impossible to imagine, for example, Jan Erlone, Mary's white boyfriend, suffocating Mary in her own bed in order to remain undetected, even though her parents emphatically disapprove of him and his Communist affiliation. But the excessiveness of Bigger's reaction is part of Wright's point. The intensity of his feelings expresses the entire set of circumstances that has shaped Bigger's response. He is seized by "hysterical terror," dominated by "frenzy," and he acts "frantically." The reason for these extreme feelings is condensed in the figure of blind Mrs. Dalton. She is the white world, deceptively fragile, but immensely threatening to the young black man, for she carries with her, for all her seeming weakness, the implacable power of a white world that hates blacks and makes them feel ashamed and guilty. Bigger is "intimidated to the core" by her as she enters. His conditioning has taught him that to be caught in the bedroom of a drunken white girl is tantamount to being convicted of rape, and rape falls under the most powerful taboo of all those that govern the relations between black and white in America. Bigger has absorbed that taboo and is terrified by its implications. . . .

VIOLENCE IS BIGGER'S AUTOMATIC RESPONSE

In Bigger's world, people make violent, not loving, physical contact. For Bigger, the alternative to aversion is violence.

In its most basic terms, *Native Son* dramatizes a bleak environment in which people touch each other only in violence, almost never in love or friendship. When Bigger remembers the moment when Jan shook his hand at their first meeting, he reflects that it was "an awful moment of hate and shame." He feels even worse later, in the car, when Mary's leg accidentally nudges him and he recoils in fear and confusion. Likewise, he is revulsed by Bessie's entire life when he places his hand on her shoulder: "It brought to him a full sense of her life, what he had been thinking and feeling when he had placed his hand upon her shoulder. The same deep realization he had that morning at home at the breakfast table while watching Vera and Buddy and his mother came back to him; only it was Bessie he was looking at now and seeing how blind she was. He felt the narrow orbit of her life. . . ." Indeed, most of the times when Bigger physically makes contact with other people result in acts of automatic violence—poking Gus with his knife, suffocating Mary, crushing Bessie's skull, and knocking out a policeman with his revolver. Even when his own family gets too close to him, he has an urge "to wave his hand and blot them out. They were always too close to him. . . ."

Robert James Butler, "The Function of Violence in Richard Wright's *Native Son*," *Black American Literature Forum*, vol. 20, no. 1–2, 1986, pp. 9–25.

Wright does not summon up this background to put us on Bigger's side. He simply asks the reader to face the full "hard and deep" horror of Bigger's act. While we may be brought to recognize the forces that shape him and lead him to the murders he commits, we must not think of him as more sinned against than sinning. He is an American black man, and he hates with a virulence that Wright daringly, for the time, insists upon acknowledging. Thus, Wright does not stop with the relatively mild scene in which Bigger smothers Mary with her pillow. To hide his crime, he must resort to greater horror. The conditions for escaping the notice of Mrs. Dalton dictated his suffocating Mary. When he gets the girl's body to the furnace room, new conditions require that he decapitate it. The blazing furnace, melodramatically evoking the fires of hell, must receive her body and become, also melodramatically, her crypt and the womb from which Bigger will emerge newly born. He does not accomplish the deed unfeelingly, or with a relish of revenge against the white race. He does it out of desperation for safety. But he is nearly overwhelmed by the frightfulness of what he is doing, by the smell of Mary's body, the blood that flows from her throat when he attempts to cut off her head with his knife. His thoughts are frantic: "He wanted to run from the basement and go as far as possible from the sight of this bloody throat. . . . He wanted to lie down upon the floor and sleep off the horror of this thing."

Bigger is not the brute of the newspaper stories. Nor is he the rolling-eyed jelly-knee of the cinema stereotype who runs from ghosts. Such creatures do not feel with Bigger's intensity—the fear, the frenzy, the frustration. His muscles as well as his will, under the Poe-esque gaze of the Daltons' white cat, are assaulted by a larger sense of guilt than the racial, and by the recoil against the physical abuse of another member of his kind. But he is impelled by the even more basic human need to save himself, which takes precedence over his revulsion at what he has done to Mary's body. Above all his horror he remembers that "he had to burn this girl . . . he had to get out of here."

BIGGER FINDS SELF-WORTH

Bigger did not plan this murder, or the grotesque means of getting rid of the body. . . .The circumstances of a racist culture put him at a certain place at a certain time and force upon him a choice that can have no safe outcome. Without time to think, Bigger reacts according to his simplest instincts. It turns out that they have not been completely determined by his social conditioning. American racial conventions require that the fear Bigger feels toward whites should cause him to think of the white taboo before anything else. When Mrs. Dalton appears, he might have collapsed in paralysis, like a minstrel Step 'n Fetchit, allowing the white world to penetrate the last protection of his sense of self-worth. Instead, he saves himself, giving priority to his own existence over the racial values of white America and conferring a value upon himself that he had never been conscious of before. In the days following the murder, Bigger gets a firmer grip on that consciousness. Waiting in his cell to be executed, he understands what he has done: "What I killed for I am." It is not until he is called upon to make the choice between himself and Mary and her world that he recognizes the worth he has put upon his own life. "It must've been pretty deep in me to make me kill," he says. "I must have felt it awful hard to murder." Only a human being who senses the fundamental immorality of murder could use the act as a measure of the intensity of his own feelings. And though he does not realize the dangerous irony in his reversal of normal values, Bigger comes to believe that through his violent act he has replaced with self-esteem the feelings of shame, guilt, and fear that have dominated his life.

His new consciousness produces a more acute sense of being present in life. With a new sense of his own importance, his need to elude detection by the white world becomes more intense, too. He learns to plan, to project, to consider the future. He becomes more finely aware of his every move, the tone of his voice, the effect he is having on others. All his senses work with an exhilarating clarity that replaces the cloudy feelings of anxiety that weighed upon his thoughts about his gang and their petty crimes. Bigger now occupies stage center, alone, singled out by the spotlight of his heightened self-consciousness and his bracing new role as a man important enough to be wanted by the police. . . .

VIOLENCE EMPOWERS BIGGER THOMAS

Precisely what the killing of Mary Dalton means to him, though, becomes fully clear only after he commits his second murder. The motive behind his killing Bessie Mears expresses his deepest need. In spite of the fear he once again feels as he brings the brick down upon her skull, after it is over and he is sure she is dead, he experiences "a queer sense of power. *He* had done this. *He* had brought all this about. In all his life these two murders were the most meaningful things that had ever happened to him. He was living, truly and deeply, no matter what others might think, looking at him with their blind eyes.". . .

Having inadvertently taken a drink of the heady liquor, Bigger craves more to sustain his high. His nerves become "hungry" to follow the newly opened avenue into a "strange land." He trembles; he gets "tremendously excited"; he anticipates more to come. Boris A. Max, his defense attorney, claims that Bigger "was impelled toward murder as much through the thirst for excitement, exultation, and elation as he was through fear! It was his way of *living*!"

Bigger is a modern paradox. Born of our civilization, he is a major threat to it. . . . He has been estranged, says Wright of Bigger, not only from the "folk," but from the past and from himself. Without work or faith or tradition to sustain him, Bigger and the "mass-man" find no soil to hold their roots or give them nourishment. They live a pale vicarious life watching others do the things they want to do. Bigger exhausts himself, says Wright, trying "to react to and answer the call of the dominant civilization whose glitter came to him through the newspapers, magazines, radios, movies, and the mere imposing sight and sound of daily American life." This is a dangerous man to society. The resentment he feels over "the balked longing for some kind of fulfillment and exultation," Max warns the judge hearing Bigger's case, "makes our future seem a looming image of violence."

BIGGER IS A CREATURE OF A NEW, VIOLENT WORLD

Part of the meaning of Bigger's violence is not only that he is a black man striking out against the boundaries of racism, but that he is a man living a key modern experience. . . .

Confronted by a sense of growing isolation, an increasing loss of self and respect for individual life, and an alienation of people from themselves, their work, and each other, the mass-man pursues violence in order to feel alive. However humanly intense Bigger's agitation is as he commits the crimes upon Mary and Bessie, it is a self-absorbed one. . . . Bigger does not identify with the living person of his victims. Mary is "not real" to him, "not a human being." This estrangement from life is the foundation of the fascist character. Bigger likes "to hear of how Japan was conquering China; of how Hitler was running the Jews to the ground; of how Mussolini was invading Spain." He thinks dimly of a dictatorship in which a black man "would whip the black people into a tight band . . . make all those black people act together, rule them, tell them what to do, and make them do it."

This is perhaps the most disturbing thing of all for Wright—the use of violence for national and self-fulfillment. Ruling black people, forcing them into a fighting instrument, would be, for Bigger, "one way to end fear and shame." Bigger's motive here is not the simple and heroic one that makes him want to go down fighting. . . . Bigger gets satisfaction from the power over others his violence gives him. It is on this basis that the dictatorships of Japan, Germany, and Italy appeal to him.

Today we speak of the "holocaust," and try to explain it. And we are still puzzling over the Moscow trials of the 1930s. Wright, without the full evidence of the ovens at Auschwitz and Buchenwald and probably unwilling to examine too closely what little news leaked out about the Communist purges, sensed something in the air of his time. He tried to combine the unformed image of some horror stalking the modern world with the well-defined image of the ghetto black man, seeing in them a dangerous similarity. Bigger was for Wright much more than a "bad nigger," or even a black revolutionary. He was a creature of the new world.

Violence in *Native Son* Shocks Readers into Awareness of White Oppression

Laurel J. Gardner

Laurel J. Gardner, a Ph.D. candidate in English at the University of South Carolina at Columbia, describes Bigger Thomas as an "animal-like creature incapable of love and capable of shocking betrayal and brutality when his life is threatened." Wright created this antihero in the hope that white readers would recoil from his violent acts in fear. Although Bigger's violence is eventually a liberating force for him, Wright's ultimate hope for the novel is that white readers will be shocked into an awareness of the ravages of racism and realize their own role in the oppression of blacks.

Richard Wright's fiction may be hard to stomach, especially for white readers. As we enter into his fictional worlds, whether they are the rural landscapes of *Uncle Tom's Children* or the urban wasteland of Chicago in *Native Son*, we experience the soul-deadening bleakness and fear that his black characters experience as they struggle, in varying degrees and ways, to protect themselves from physical and psychic death. In Wright's fiction, nearly all whites hate blacks and they oppress them in order to wring money out of them. Russell Carl Brignano argues that "Wright implies in both novels [*Native Son* and *Lawd Today*] that framing the superstructure of society dominated by the white world is capitalism, which is a force that smothers and denies the individual personality." In a capitalist world governed by whites who have no desire to share their power or wealth and who oppress blacks through intimidation and humilia-

Excerpted from "The Progression of Meaning in the Images of Violence in Richard Wright's *Uncle Tom's Children* and *Native Son*," by Laurel J. Gardner, *College Language Association Journal*, vol. 38, no. 4, 1995. Reprinted with permission from the *College Language Association Journal*.

tion, blacks must either give up their dreams, assuaging themselves with religion or alcohol, or strike back in acts of violence, the only recourse left to blacks who refuse to give up. According to Brignano, "what Wright . . . resented in the Southern Negro psyche . . . [was] an 'Uncle Tom' submissiveness to one's lot." For Wright, physical violence was a natural and inevitable way to affirm one's self and dignity in response to hatred and oppression. Ranging from frightened, accidental acts of murder in *Uncle Tom's Children* to Bigger's premeditated murder of his girlfriend in *Native Son*, Wright employs a progression of violent acts to show a range of courage and will to assert selfhood in his oppressed black protagonists. . . .

BIGGER IS A PRODUCT OF HIS ENVIRONMENT

In *Native Son*, Wright forged a new character from the black protagonists of *Uncle Tom's Children* and the blacks he had known from his own experience growing up in ghettos. No longer content to show blacks as pathetic victims of white hatred, Wright created a character who represents the evil that the white world creates in its oppression of blacks. Moving his literary setting from the rural South to the urban North, Wright placed his new protagonist in the world of capitalism, urban poverty, and racial segregation. In this hopelessly circumscribed world of opportunities, shut off from the world of possibilities of human development and accomplishment, starved of true familial love and understanding, and suffering the palpable presence of white hatred and oppression every day, Bigger reaches adulthood consumed by a profound and seemingly boundless fear and hatred of the white world he does not understand. In this bleak milieu, we watch Bigger begin to act on his feelings, thus for the first time asserting his selfhood and taking control of his life by committing horrendous acts of violence before the wrath of the dominant culture descends on him and snuffs him out. By portraying Bigger as an animal-like creature incapable of love and capable of shocking betrayal and brutality when his life is threatened, Wright guaranteed that his largely white liberal audience would recoil in disgust and fear. Yet by allowing us to see into Bigger's psyche and come to understand his feelings and motivations, Wright causes us to realize that Bigger is merely the tragic and dangerous product of his environment. Given that he is circumscribed by white wealth and authority, his powerful will to live asserts itself in the only way that remains—by attacking viciously anybody who threatens him.

Wright examines Bigger's acts of violence in much more psychological depth than he does the violence in *Uncle Tom's Children*. The blacks in his earlier short stories, with the exception of Reverend Taylor in "Fire and Cloud," act violently in self-defense to a direct assault from whites; then they perish or disappear almost immediately. In *Native Son*, however, we witness Bigger grow psychologically and emotionally from his murders. We are shown that in the perverted world of white oppression of blacks, the only avenue left for blacks to claim authority and control over their lives is through violence. And the atrocious nature of Bigger's crimes reveals the enormity of the crimes that whites commit against blacks. . . .

Much of the violence in *Native Son*, with the important exception of the murder of Bessie, occurs in Book One, "Fear." As many critics have noted, the novel opens with Bigger killing a large rat in the tiny slum apartment which he shares with his mother, brother, and sister. Bigger enjoys killing the rat, but he becomes connected with the rat, which represents his existence. As Brignano explains, "The action [of chasing and killing the rat] is ironically symbolic. Later Bigger will assume the role of a hunted animal, and the rat will be interchanged in the minds of the whites with Negroes in general." Yet another crucial element of this scene is that it reveals the cruelty in Bigger. He waves the bloody dead rat in the face of his terrified sister: "Bigger laughed and approached the bed with the dangling rat, swinging it to and fro like a pendulum, enjoying his sister's fear." Wright immediately undercuts the pity we feel for Bigger and his family living in such squalid and unhealthy surroundings by showing us Bigger's meanness. Yet he also tempers that exposure of the smallness of Bigger's nature with an insight into its source: "He hated his family because he knew that they were suffering and that he was powerless to help them. He knew that the moment he allowed himself to feel to its fullness how they lived, the shame and misery of their lives, he would be swept out of himself with fear and despair." Throughout the novel Wright balances the grisly viciousness of Bigger's violent actions with deep insight, usually framed in the narrator's eloquent language, into the reasons behind

Bigger's actions. We are shown over and over, as John Reilly wrote in the afterword to the novel, that "violence is a personal necessity for the oppressed."

A LIFETIME OF HUMILIATION ENDS IN VIOLENCE

When Bigger leaves his apartment, we learn how profoundly angry and fearful he is. . . . Bigger tells his friend Gus that when he thinks about how whites "don't let us do *nothing*," he feels "like somebody's poking a red-hot iron down my throat." A little later he tells Gus, "Every time I think of 'em, I *feel* 'em. . . . It's like fire. . . . It's like I was going to do something I can't help." Not only does Bigger hate whites, but he is deeply afraid of them. He plans to rob a white man's store with his friends, their first robbery of whites, but he is so terrified of acting on his hatred of whites that he picks a fight with Gus. It is essential to his survival that he not give in to his fear. He is dimly aware that "his courage to live depended upon how successfully his fear was hidden from his consciousness." He reveals again an even worse cruelty when he forces Gus to lick the knife blade that he points at his throat: "Bigger held the open blade an inch from Gus's lips. 'Lick it,' Bigger said, his body tingling with elation. Gus's eyes filled with tears. 'Lick it, I said! You think I'm playing?'" When the barkeeper stops the fight with a gun, Bigger slashes the felt on the pool table on his way out. In these opening scenes we see that Bigger is no pitiable victim. . . . Instead Wright made Bigger a nasty, even frightening young black man who has the potential to explode in violence, but of whom we are developing a tentative understanding.

Although we are intellectually prepared for Bigger's murder of Mary Dalton, we are not emotionally prepared for the shocking nature of the disposal of her body. Bigger murders Mary not so much because of the exigencies of the immediate situation in which he might be caught transgressing the most sacred taboo—that of sexual relations between a black man and a white woman—but because of a lifetime of accumulated humiliation and intimidation by whites. When Jan insists that Bigger shake hands with him, something Bigger has never done with a white man before, he is convulsed with hate: "He felt naked, transparent; he felt that this white man, having helped to put him down, having helped to deform him, held him up now to look at him and be amused. At that moment he felt toward Mary and Jan a dumb, cold, and inarticulate hate." Just as the whites refuse to see Bigger as an individual human being, Bigger sees Jan and Mary as representations of that same vague white blur of which all whites are a part in Bigger's eyes. Although Bigger is innocent of premeditated murder and literal rape, as he reflects later, his murder of Mary is but an embodiment of the countless desires to murder and rape which he experienced before: "Though he had killed by accident, not once did he feel the need to tell himself that it had been an accident. . . . And in a certain sense he knew that the girl's death had not been accidental. He had killed many times before, only on those other times there had been no handy victim or circumstance to make visible or dramatic his will to kill."

THE NOVEL'S IRONY: BIGGER IS LIBERATED THROUGH VIOLENCE

After Bigger murders Mary, he undergoes a profound transformation. He awakes to a world blanketed by snow, a visual symbol of white pervasiveness and power. He also sees his family and himself in an existential light: "He looked round the room, seeing it for the first time. . . . He hated this room and all the people in it, including himself. . . . Maybe they had to live this way precisely because none of them in all their lives had ever done anything, right or wrong, that mattered much." He begins to become consciously aware that he cannot accept his mother's withdrawal into religion or the passivity of his brother and sister. The force of his will, his sense of himself, his refusal to accept the annihilation of any possibility of forging a self in interaction with the world, all these factors push Bigger towards violence. And when he realizes that he has accomplished what he feared most, when he realizes that he has murdered a white woman, he is elated that he conquered his fear enough to act. Because only through overcoming our fears and daring to act may we become human. The horrifying irony is that Bigger's actions can only entail violence; he cannot join the Navy, he cannot learn to fly a plane, as he wishes, he cannot do anything except the most menial manual labor and live in a cramped hovel that denies each inhabitant human dignity. It is only natural and understandable that he is elated at having murdered Mary: "He felt that he had his destiny in his grasp. . . . What his knife and gun had once meant to him, his knowledge of having secretly murdered Mary now meant." He enjoys a confidence in his relations with his family and friends that he never experienced before.

Juxtaposed against the new Bigger who is somewhat liberated from a torturous fear, for whom we may feel some faint flickers of happiness, are revelations that Bigger is capable of killing again, and no one is safe from him if they represent even the slightest threat to his safety. Again, Wright undercuts any sympathetic identification with Bigger that the reader may develop with deeper insights into Bigger's monstrousness. We see that Bigger is capable of killing his brother, the young boy who fawns after him like a puppy. Bigger thinks to himself, "He had felt toward Buddy for an instant as he had felt toward Mary when she lay upon the bed with the white blur moving toward him in the hazy blue light of the room. But he won't tell, he thought." And just as chilling is his blaming of Mary for her own murder. As do many psychopaths, Bigger blames his victim for getting in his way: "Hell, she *made* me do it! I couldn't help it! She should've known better! She should've left me alone, goddammit! . . . He felt that his murder of her was more than amply justified by the fear and shame she had made him feel." And once again, we see his complete readiness to kill when he talks to the Daltons' maid Peggy: "Quickly, he wondered if he would have to kill her [Peggy] to keep her from telling if she turned on the light and saw something that made her think that Mary was dead."

Just as we were intellectually prepared but emotionally unprepared for the murder of Mary, we are shocked by the nearly unspeakable loathsomeness of his rape and murder of his own girlfriend Bessie, though Wright has prepared us for the crime by showing that Bigger is ready to kill Peggy or even his own adoring brother if either should jeopardize his safety. Yet lest we entertain even the slightest glimmer of belief that Bigger might operate with morals similar to others or might feel loyalty to those with whom he has been closest, Wright depicts Bigger planning to murder Bessie when he is in her apartment. And what is worse is that knowing that he will kill her, and even having already spotted a handy brick to use as a murder weapon, Bigger satisfies his sexual needs with her while mentally blocking out her protestations. Then, after she has fallen asleep, he smashes her head to a bloody pulp, throws her body down an airshaft, and goes to sleep. Although Bigger is capable of feeling guilt—as he does when he looks Jan in the eye and sees Jan's confusion at being accused, and when he thinks of looking at Bessie's face after he has killed her—this guilt is not powerful enough to keep him from hurting those who pose, even in their innocence, a threat to his survival. In fact, the pain of feeling guilt could drive him to kill again. We see how dangerous his experience of guilt could be when he talks with Jan soon after the murder: "He felt that if Jan continued to stand there and make him feel this awful sense of guilt, he would have to shoot him in spite of himself." Bigger will kill to protect his psychic survival as well as his physical survival.

WRIGHT'S ULTIMATE GOAL IS TO
SHOCK READERS INTO AWARENESS

The critic Alan W. France has shown in a very interesting and compelling essay the misogyny behind Bigger's crime. He states that this feminist reading is at odds with both the narrator's presentation of the crimes and Wright's statement of his intentions in his introduction as being racially motivated. He shows how Bigger's intimidation of Gus is a "symbolic rape-slaying," similar to the underlying sexual tension in Mary's murder. The rape-murder of Bessie, of course, is blatant. France underscores the sexual aggression involved in the act of murdering Bessie: "Only the inscription of the text identifies the blunt instrument that 'plunged downward . . . landed with a thud . . . lifted again and again . . . in falling . . . struck a sodden mass that gave softly but stoutly to each landing blow . . . seemed to be striking a wet wad of cotton . . . the jarring impact' as the weapon of the murder and not the rape." France argues that the novel is really about how men see women as commodities in a capitalist world, and because Bigger is "marginalized and dehumanized," he seeks revenge by destroying the property of his capitalist oppressor and feels free to destroy his own property as well, for "except for his knife and gun, Bessie is the only property Bigger has ever possessed." According to France, "the novel grows out of this suppressed interrelationship in which value is conferred according to property arrangements, and status is a phallic prerogative assigned by access to and ownership of commodities, including women."

Even though feminist critics may argue that misogyny is at the deepest level of the novel (after all, Bigger does hack off Mary's head and bash in Bessie's head, the centers of their intelligence and selves, reducing them to bodies without minds even in death), I do not believe that we can ignore authorial intention completely. As the more traditional critics claim, Wright created *Native Son* to shock the white reading public into an awareness of the black situation. He did not want bankers' daughters to simply cry in pity for the blacks who suffer; he wanted those emblems of privileged capitalism to be shocked into an awareness of the naiveté and condescension behind their concern for blacks as well as their own complicity in the oppression of blacks. And what better way to shock and drive home a point than to use graphic images of violence? Not only does Mary's bloody, severed head haunt Bigger; it haunts the reader. And as Reilly points out in the afterword, Wright was an angry, potentially violent man, who, as he matured, "channeled a violent and terrifying outrage into a book which forces us to experience the truth about what man does to man." Once having come to understand Bigger, sensitive readers can recognize shades of Bigger in the people around us, if not in ourselves, which is a tribute to the genius of Wright.

Chronology

1908

Richard Wright is born on September 4 in Roxie, Mississippi. Wright's father, Nathan, is a sharecropper, and his mother, Ella, is a schoolteacher.

1910

Richard's brother, Leon, is born September 24.

1911–1912

The Wright family moves to Natchez to live with Ella's mother. Richard sets fire to his grandmother's house, then hides beneath the house to avoid punishment. He later writes about this incident in great detail in *Black Boy*.

1913–1914

After their move to Memphis, Tennessee, Richard's father deserts the family for another woman. Ella works as a cook to support the family, and Richard becomes a drunkard at age six.

1916

Richard attends school for the first time, but he must drop out to care for his sick mother. She is forced to put Richard and his brother in an orphanage for more than a month because she cannot care for them. Eventually the boys move in with their maternal grandparents in Jackson, Mississippi, and then with Wright's Aunt Maggie and Uncle Silas Hoskins in Elaine, Arkansas.

1917

Richard's Uncle Hoskins is murdered by whites, another incident in *Black Boy*.

1918–1919

Moving frequently after the death of Silas Hoskins, the Wrights settle again with Ella's mother in Jackson. Richard again leaves his grandmother's house and moves with his brother and mother to West Helena, where Ella suffers a stroke. The boys are then split up among relatives, and Ella returns to her mother's.

1920

Richard attends the Seventh-Day Adventist school in Huntsville, Mississippi. He clashes with his Aunt Addie, the devoutly religious teacher of his class.

1921–1922

Richard enters fifth grade in Jackson and is soon advanced to sixth grade. He delivers newspapers and works with a traveling insurance salesman, two jobs he recalls with some shame in his autobiography.

1922–1923

Richard enters the seventh grade at the Smith-Robertson Public School and earns money for books, food, and clothes by running errands for whites. He develops an interest in pulp fiction and magazine stories.

1923–1924

During his eighth-grade year Richard writes his first short story, "The Voodoo of Hell's Half-Acre," which is published in the black newspaper *Jackson Southern Register.*

1925

In May Richard graduates valedictorian of his ninth-grade class. He resolves to forgo public education and leave the Deep South for Memphis, Tennessee.

1926

Richard works at the Merry Optical Company in Memphis in addition to other odd jobs. He begins to read extensively.

1927–1928

Richard's mother and brother join him for a short time in Memphis and then he moves on to Chicago with his Aunt Maggie. Richard works for the postal service, but fails the physical exam required to work there full-time. He spends a lot of time writing during the day.

1929

Richard gains enough weight to pass the postal health exam and begins work as a substitute clerk and mail sorter. He is writing regularly and attending meetings of black literary groups.

1930

Richard loses his postal job after the stock market crash. He works for a short time selling burial insurance to blacks, but he is dismayed by the dishonesty of the profession.

1931

Now on state relief, Richard works for the Michael Reese Hospital and later the South Side Boy's Club and Federal Negro Theatre. Richard's second publication, the short story "Superstition," appears in *Abbott's Monthly Magazine*, a black journal. During this time, Richard gains an interest in Communist activity in the African American community.

1932

Richard works as an insurance salesman and a street cleaner and moves with his family into a tenement. He attends meetings of the John Reed Club, a Communist literary group, and begins to regularly publish poems and short stories in leftist journals.

1934

Richard joins the Communist Party and is elected executive secretary of the Chicago John Reed Club.

1935

Richard goes to New York for the American Writers' Congress, where he speaks on "The Isolation of the Negro Writer." He is hired by the Federal Writers' Project to research the history of Illinois and of the Negro in Chicago.

1936

Richard organizes the Communist Party–sponsored National Negro Congress and continues to write extensively. His short story "Big Boy Leaves Home" appears in the *New Caravan* anthology, where it attracts critical attention.

1937

Richard turns down a permanent position with the postal service to move to New York City to pursue his writing career. He becomes the Harlem editor of the *Daily Worker* and helps launch the magazine *New Challenge*. His literary reputation begins to grow.

1938

Richard's book *Uncle Tom's Children: Four Novellas* is published to wide acclaim. The book receives a literary prize from *Story* magazine. He is romantically interested in Dhimah Rose Meadman, a white classical dancer, and Ellen Poplar, a white member of the Communist Party.

1939

Richard receives a Guggenheim fellowship, completes *Native Son*, and marries Dhimah Rose Meadman.

1940

Native Son is published and receives national attention after being offered as a Book-of-the-Month Club selection. Richard is estranged from wife Dhimah and begins divorce proceedings. The success of his novel affords him his first taste of financial independence.

1941

Richard marries Ellen Poplar. *Twelve Million Black Voices: A Folk History of the Negro in the United States* is published, and *Native Son* is produced on Broadway.

1942

Wright's daughter Julia is born.

1944

Wright breaks from the Communist Party and publishes a two-part article in the *Atlantic Monthly* titled "I Tried to Be a Communist."

1945

Black Boy: A Record of Childhood and Youth, Wright's autobiography, is published and, like *Native Son*, is selected by the Book-of-the-Month Club.

1946

Wright visits France for the first time and feels at home in Paris.

1947

Wright's works are translated into several European languages. He decides to move his family to France permanently.

1949

Wright's second daughter, Rachel, is born in January. He finishes a screenplay of *Native Son* and decides to play the lead character, Bigger Thomas, himself. He is unable to interest Hollywood in the script.

1950

Financial difficulties delay the filming of *Native Son* in Argentina, but the project is completed in June.

1951

Native Son opens in Buenos Aires; thirty minutes of the film are cut by censors for the U.S. premiere on June 16. The film is not well received in America.

1953

Wright's book *The Outsider* is published to mixed reviews. He visits the Gold Coast (Ghana) to gather material for his book *Black Power*.

1954

Black Power: A Record of Reactions in a Land of Pathos is published, along with *Savage Holiday*, Wright's only novel with all white characters. He visits Spain to gather material for another writing project.

1955

Wright attends the Bandung Conference in Indonesia and meets with numerous world leaders to discuss Third World problems.

1956

Wright publishes *The Color Curtain: A Report on the Bandung Conference* and *Pagan Spain*, based on his travels in Spain. He begins a lecture tour of several European countries.

1957

White Man, Listen! a collection of Wright's lectures, is published.

1958

Wright's novel *The Long Dream*, the first in a projected trilogy about Mississippi, is published. The book receives poor reviews and does not sell well. When Wright attempts to renew his passport, he is harassed by the American embassy for his former Communist associations.

1959

Wright's mother dies January 14. In June, Wright suffers from amoebic dysentery.

1960

A stage adaptation of *The Long Dream* opens on Broadway in February but closes in a week after poor reviews. Wright prepares more than eight hundred of his haiku for publication and begins work on a new novel. *Eight Men,* a collection of short stories, is also ready for publication. On November 28, Wright dies of a heart attack at age fifty-two; he is cremated with a copy of *Black Boy* on December 3 in Paris.

FOR FURTHER RESEARCH

BIOGRAPHIES

David Bakish, *Richard Wright*. New York: Frederick Ungar, 1973.

Michel Fabre, *The Unfinished Quest of Richard Wright*. Trans. Isabel Barzun. New York: William Morrow, 1973.

Robert Felgar, *Richard Wright*. Boston: Twayne, 1980.

Addison Gayle, *Richard Wright: Ordeal of a Native Son*. New York: Anchor Press, 1980.

Keneth Kinnamon, *The Emergence of Richard Wright*. Urbana: University of Illinois Press, 1972.

Margaret Walker, *Richard Wright: Demonic Genius*. New York: Warner, 1988.

CRITICISM

Richard Abcarian, *Richard Wright's* Native Son: *A Critical Handbook*. Belmont, CA: Wadsworth, 1970.

Evelyn Gross Avery, *Rebels and Victims: The Fiction of Richard Wright and Bernard Malamud*. New York: Kennikat Press, 1979.

Harold Bloom, ed., *Bigger Thomas*. New York: Chelsea House, 1990.

——, *Richard Wright*. New York: Chelsea House, 1987.

Yoshinobu Hakutani, ed., *Critical Essays on Richard Wright*. Boston: G.K. Hall, 1982.

——, *Richard Wright and Racial Discourse*. Columbia: University of Missouri Press, 1996.

Keneth Kinnamon, ed., *Critical Essays on Richard Wright's* Native Son. New York: Twayne, 1997.

————, "How *Native Son* Was Born." In James Barbour, ed., *Writing the American Classics*. Chapel Hill: University of North Carolina Press, 1990.

————, *New Essays on* Native Son. New York: Cambridge University Press, 1990.

Arnold Rampersad, ed., *Richard Wright: A Collection of Critical Essays*. Englewood Cliffs, NJ: Prentice-Hall, 1995.

John M. Reilly, ed., *Richard Wright: The Critical Reception*. New York: B. Franklin, 1978.

AFRICAN AMERICAN AUTOBIOGRAPHY AND HISTORY

William L. Andrews, ed., *African American Autobiography: A Collection of Critical Essays*. New Century Views Series. Englewood Cliffs, NJ: Prentice-Hall, 1993.

Ira Berlin, ed., *Remembering Slavery: African Americans Talk About Their Personal Experiences of Slavery and Freedom*. New York: Norton, 1998.

John Hope Franklin, *From Slavery to Freedom: A History of African Americans*. New York: Knopf, 1994.

Henry Louis Gates, ed., *Colored People: A Memoir*. New York: Knopf, 1994.

Leon F. Litwack, *Trouble in Mind: Black Southerners in the Age of Jim Crow*. New York: Knopf, 1998.

Crispin Sartwell, *Act Like You Know: African-American Autobiography and White Identity*. Chicago: University of Illinois Press, 1998.

Jeffrey C. Stewart, *1001 Things Everyone Should Know About African American History*. New York: Doubleday, 1997.

AFRICAN AMERICAN LITERATURE

Bernard W. Bell, *The Afro-American Novel and Its Tradition*. Amherst: University of Massachusetts Press, 1989.

Robert Butler, *Contemporary African American Fiction: The Open Journey*. Madison, NJ: Fairleigh Dickinson University Press, 1998.

Michael G. Cooke, *Afro-American Literature in the Twentieth Century: The Achievement of Intimacy*. New Haven, CT: Yale University Press, 1986.

Henry Louis Gates, ed., *The Norton Anthology of African American Literature.* New York: Norton, 1997.

Carl Milton Hughes, *The Negro Novelist: A Discussion of the Writings of American Negro Novelists 1940–1950.* New York: Citadel Press, 1994.

Charles Richard Johnson, *Being and Race: Black Writing Since 1970.* Bloomington: Indiana University Press, 1988.

INDEX